Advance Praise for *Go Further, Faster*

'Lulu's book *Go Further, Faster* offers many of her direct and honest learnings from her esteemed career at Landor. By looking back and "connecting the dots" in a very conversational way, she's written the perfect guide book for young professionals wanting a head-start on "shaping a life that matters".'

Angela Ahrendts DBE, former Chief Executive Officer, Burberry, and former Senior Vice President, Apple Retail

'*Go Further, Faster* is a testament to Lulu Raghavan's journey of growth, resilience and ambition in an environment dominated by men. Having mentored Lulu and witnessed her evolution first-hand, I can confidently say that her insights are invaluable for any woman seeking to carve her own path in the professional world. This book is a treasure trove of practical advice, real-life examples and heartfelt encouragement. It brilliantly captures Lulu's unique blend of optimism, realism and tenacity, making it an essential read for ambitious women everywhere. If you're looking to accelerate your career while maintaining a fulfilling personal life, this book is your roadmap.'

Jane Geraghty, Chief Client Officer, WPP, and Chairman, Landor

'This book is full of nuggets of wisdom for anyone just starting their career or wanting to kick-start their professional journey. The tenets of working on yourself, lifting as you climb and having a learning mindset to become the best version of yourself are all ones I firmly believe in. It's all about the importance of self-belief, resilience, goal setting, mentoring, listening and networking. Lulu's phrase "humbition" – the need for ambition but always acting with humility – is spot on. This is a great read!'

Leena Nair, Chief Executive Officer, Chanel

'It is wonderful to see Lulu pay it forward by helping others who have the ambition and need the inspiration. *Go Further, Faster* is a valuable resource for personal and professional growth, offering insights and strategies to navigate the complexities of the modern workplace. Her conversational style and practical tips make this a very relevant read for those looking to jumpstart their careers.'

Shantanu Narayen, Chair and Chief Executive Officer, Adobe Systems

'*Go Further, Faster* is not just a guide – it's a beacon of light for those navigating the modern workplace. Lulu's blend of practical advice and inspirational anecdotes equips readers with the tools they need to build their dream careers and lead fulfilling lives. Readers will discover that the sky is the limit when they have the courage to chase their dreams and bet boldly on themselves. Whether you're aiming to climb the corporate ladder or make a meaningful impact in your community, this book is a great companion on your journey to success.'

Falguni Nayar, Founder and Chief Executive Officer, Nykaa

'I've had the great pleasure of working with Lulu for many years as she charted her remarkable career at Landor. It is very heartening to see her share her invaluable insights with the next generation through *Go Further, Faster*. I'm sure this book will be a source of great wisdom and learning for those who want to emulate Lulu and thrive in corporate life while maintaining a balance with their personal goals.'

Anand Mahindra, Chairman, Mahindra Group

'This book is an invaluable guide for young women professionals who aspire to achieve their full potential and shatter all the glass ceilings they encounter along the way. Lulu Raghavan draws on her rich career and life experience to distil simple, powerful and practical learnings that strike a chord. From developing character skills to leading a fulfilling life, from building your personal brand to contributing to the world around you, these pages are full of learning and insight.'

Harish Bhat, former Brand Custodian, Tata Sons, and bestselling author

'All of us spend our lives working, earning and saving – do I refer to money and wealth? No, I refer to personal and professional experiences, which are contextual and carry life lessons. One can share financial wealth as one wishes. But it is hugely wasteful to carry "experiential wealth" to the final place. Read the book, savour it and find inspiration to write your story too. This book is remarkable for more reasons than just one.'

R. Gopalakrishnan, author and corporate commentator

'Lulu Raghavan's *Go Further, Faster* is a roadmap for young women stepping into the world of work. In today's fast-paced environment, navigating the nuances of career advancement while maintaining a fulfilling personal life can be daunting. The book addresses these challenges head on, offering practical advice and insightful wisdom from her own experiences. As someone who works with a team of women and has had the privilege of mentoring them too, I have no doubt that this book will inspire and empower countless women to reach their full potential, creating the careers and lives they envision for themselves!'

Pooja Dhingra, Founder and Chief Executive Officer, Le 15 Patisserie

'Written in a conversational style, Lulu's book is full of practical wisdom. For a young leader, if you just take the chapters on reading and writing to heart, it will set you up for life. I took away many things I can implement, including some new book recommendations!'

Dr Ranjan Banerjee, Vice-Chancellor and Professor, Nayanta University, and former Dean, S.P. Jain Institute of Management and Research

'Lulu hasn't just "been there and done that", she is there and doing it. Lulu isn't just a leader, she leads. Every day she opens doors for others and holds them open as they walk through. This book will open even more doors for us all.'

Julia Middleton, Founder, Women Emerging UK, and Founder and former Chief Executive Officer, Common Purpose

'As Brand Custodian of Godrej, I know first-hand the immense value of a strong brand to a business. Lulu, who has been a brand evangelist for years and who I've worked with as a consultant, has taken all her learnings on brand from her impressive career at Landor to shape a unique perspective on how individuals can build their own personal brands to creative competitive advantage for themselves at the workplace. Lulu's book is particularly relevant to young professionals looking to make a mark as soon as possible.'

Tanya Dubash, Executive Director and Chief Brand Officer, Godrej Group

'Lulu has served as a mentor for our SVA Masters in Branding programme for over seven years now. I'm thrilled to see her widen the scope of her impact on young professionals through her book in which she has drawn on life lessons to share from her career in branding and design at Landor as well as her personal development journey as a leader. Lulu's career trajectory shows that with passion, ambition and drive, you can achieve more than you can imagine.'

Debbie Millman, host, Design Matters, Editorial Director, Print Magazine, and Chair, Masters in Branding, School of Visual Arts

Go Further, Faster

GO FURTHER, FASTER

Shaping a Life That Matters

Lulu Raghavan

Foreword by P.V. Sindhu

BLOOMSBURY
NEW DELHI • LONDON • OXFORD • NEW YORK • SYDNEY

BLOOMSBURY INDIA
Bloomsbury Publishing India Pvt. Ltd
Second Floor, LSC Building No. 4, DDA Complex, Pocket C – 6 & 7,
Vasant Kunj, New Delhi, 110070

BLOOMSBURY, BLOOMSBURY INDIA and the Diana logo
are trademarks of Bloomsbury Publishing Plc

First published in India 2024
This edition published 2024

ISBN: PB: 978-93-56405-57-8; eBook: 978-93-56405-58-5
2 4 6 8 10 9 7 5 3 1

Typeset in Bembo Std by Manipal Technologies Limited
Printed and bound in India by Thomson Press India Ltd

To my parents, Dr Sheilu Sreenivasan and Gopal Srinivasan
For their unconditional love, always.

To my husband, Harsha Raghavan
For challenging me to rise to my highest potential, always.

To my darling daughters, Ruhi and Riva Raghavan
For being my biggest cheerleaders, always.

Contents

Foreword by P.V. Sindhu xv
Why I Wrote This Book xvii

PART I: DEVELOP YOURSELF

1. Mind 3
   Engaging with Reading 3
   Embracing Silence 8
   Self-Awareness 11
   Journaling 13
   Writing 17
   Management of Your Mind 21
   Time Management 26
   Connecting the Dots 34
   Building Resilience 37
   Goal Orientation 40
   Achievement, Not Activity 41
   Developing Range 43
   Feedback 45

2. Body 48
   Breathing Techniques 50
   Managing Your Energy 53
   Restful Sleep 56
   Nutrition 59
   Physical Fitness 65

3. Soul 72
   Gratitude 72
   Empathy 76
   Emotional Intelligence 78
   Personal Relationships 82

Professional Relationships 84
Cultivating Joy 87
Leading a Psychologically Rich Life 88
Authenticity and Vulnerability 92
Be a 'Lovecat' 96
Be Kind, Always 98

PART 2: PROMOTE YOURSELF

4. Act 1: Discover 115
5. Act 2: Define 122
6. Act 3: Design 130
7. Act 4: Deploy 137
8. Act 5: Deliver 150

PART 3: EVOLVE YOURSELF

9. Continuous Growth and Development 159
Becoming a Lifelong Learner 159
Humbition 162
Become a Great Listener 166
Negotiation 169

10. Helping Others Rise as You Rise 171
Celebrating Others 171
Managing Comparison 173
Leading with Compassion 175
Mentoring 178

11. Broadening Your Influence 181
Industry Events 181
Corporate Boards 182
Nonprofits 182

PART 4: HANDY HOW-TOS

How to Ace a Job Interview 187
How to Say No 190
How to Build a Tribe 192

How to Disagree with Bosses and Colleagues 193
How to Ask for Anything 195
How to Overcome Limiting Self-Beliefs 196
How to Handle Rejection 199
How to Overcome Internal Barriers to Success 200

Conclusion 205

Acknowledgements 211
About My Professional Journey 213
Index 221
About the Author 225

Foreword

AS AN ATHLETE, I know that success is not just about physical strength and skill. It also requires mental toughness, emotional intelligence and a drive to continuously improve oneself. That's why I was drawn to Lulu Raghavan's book, *Go Further, Faster: Shaping a Life That Matters*.

In this book, Lulu offers practical advice on how to develop yourself, promote yourself and evolve yourself to achieve your goals and live a fulfilling life. She covers topics such as mind management, time management, resilience, goal orientation and achievement. As someone who has faced many challenges and setbacks, I can attest to the importance of these skills.

Lulu also emphasises the importance of taking care of your body through breathing, managing energy, sleep, nutrition, and physical exercise. As an athlete, I know first-hand how crucial it is to maintain a healthy body to perform at your best.

But Lulu doesn't stop there. She also delves into the soulful aspects of life, such as gratitude, empathy, emotional intelligence, personal and professional relationships, and cultivating joy. These are all essential components of a well-rounded and fulfilling life.

The second part of the book focuses on promoting yourself, with actionable steps on how to discover, define, design, deploy, and deliver your goals.

In the third part, Lulu discusses the importance of continuous growth and development, helping others rise as you rise, and broadening your influence.

Throughout the book, Lulu provides handy how-tos on topics such as asking for a raise, acing a job interview, building a tribe and handling rejection. These practical tips are invaluable for anyone looking to advance their career or personal life. I was particularly impressed by Lulu's emphasis on the importance of continuous growth and development. As she says, 'There is no destination that you are striving to reach. Rather, you are always on a continuous journey of learning and evolution.' This is something that I have always believed in, and it is a message that I would encourage all young women to take to heart.

So my shout out to every reader is: With *Go Further, Faster*, the world is yours to conquer!!!

P.V. Sindhu
Two-time Olympic medallist and
India's first women's world champion in badminton

Why I Wrote This Book

IT WAS A HOT summer day in Mumbai in 2015. My colleague Gazala and I had set up our laptop in a makeshift conference room at the NSCI centre. We were all set to conduct a workshop on personal branding for attendees of the Zee MELT Conference. As we waited, fifteen minutes before the event was to start, not a single person had arrived. We wondered if the topic was boring or if we lacked star power as speakers. The air-conditioner blasted cool air and we wished we had brought sweaters.

In a matter of ten minutes, the scene changed dramatically. We were starting to perspire. The room not only filled up entirely but the temporary doors were opened wider to allow standing room. The workshop was oversubscribed and instead of thirty, we had over fifty enthusiastic participants waiting to see what we had to say. People took pictures of slides. Many came up to me after the session to express gratitude.

There were a few key messages we wanted to land with the audience: i) you need to take time and effort to nurture your personal brand just as you would nurture the brands you work on; ii) you can't sit in a corner beavering away and expect your work to be recognised; iii) you have to build your own brand and you have to do it 'by design' and not 'by default.' All three struck a deep chord with this predominantly advertising and marketing audience.

That was the first time I knew I was on to something with this topic of personal branding. But I knew that personal branding was just the tip of the iceberg. It should be done after you have developed yourself sufficiently in all aspects. The savvier ones in the audience understood this but I did not want the message to be lost on everyone else. I had to ensure that people don't think that personal branding is cosmetic. They need to understand that it goes much deeper than shouting from the rooftop.

As I started getting more speaking opportunities on personal branding, I kept developing my thoughts and recommendations to embrace a more holistic inside-out approach to professional and personal growth and development. The Q&A sessions with various audiences helped me understand their aspirations as well as their anxieties. Young women were my most ardent fans, especially those who may not have had exposure to many of these ideas in their upbringing. They lacked relatable role models and easy-to-follow guidance. I noticed that they were lapping up the tips I was sharing. My messages were resonating resoundingly.

It struck me that these young women who were connecting with my journey and my messages have a burning desire to become successful, but they lack the proper guidance for propelling themselves through the corporate world. Once they join the workplace it may be too late. The sink or swim environment can be too deep an ocean if you are not prepared. Some may be lucky to have access to professional corporate training programmes in which some elements I talk about are covered. What about the rest? How would they pick the mindset, the habits and the tools that can be so valuable to career growth?

Seeing this opportunity to nurture young women in the workplace, I briefly flirted with the idea of quitting my job and launching my own venture dedicated to mentoring young women to rise and shine. But I love my job, my company, my colleagues, and the global opportunities I have at Landor. I needed another way in which I could make a positive difference in the lives of these hugely talented and ambitious young women I was meeting every day.

At the same time, another thought was niggling me. I was preaching to the audience that they needed to invest in their personal website to tell their story to the world. This would help them build a distinct personal brand. I hadn't done that for myself. I did not want to be disingenuous or be called out for not taking my own medicine!

This is when I conceptualised, designed, and launched my own website (https://luluraghavan.com/). Indrajit Gupta (former editor of *Fortune India* who I had met a few years earlier at an SPJIMR alumni gathering and had kept in touch with) suggested that I start a newsletter to build a community. He advised me that this could be a good way to cultivate a digital audience, ahead of potentially writing a book in a few years. That's how my weekly newsletter *Ideas to Play With* was born as a key part of my website's content. Each week I touched upon a theme related to personal growth. The goal was to ignite the curiosity of my subscribers and make them want to learn more on their own

Once my website was done, my good friend Pavithra pushed me to get started on writing a book. She suggested that I get a writing coach. Quite serendipitously, Chinmayee Manjunath (who helped my friend Srimoyi Bhattacharya publish her first book, *Pitch Perfect*) replied to one of my stories on Instagram. I expressed my desire to work with her on a book and, *voila*, here we are.

I'm writing this book as the one I wish I had read when I was starting my career. Whether it is the importance of being a lifelong learner, the need to navigate corporate politics with diplomacy, the devastating health impact of workaholism or the why and how of building a personal brand, there are so many things I wish I had known when I was younger. It may have accelerated my opportunities for advancement or presented paths that I hadn't envisioned.

There are three parts to my book.

Part 1 is the longest. I talk about the holistic development of yourself. I'll cover approaches to mind, body and soul development. I believe that you must take great care of all three to have a flourishing career.

Part 2 is about promoting yourself. This is how to shape yourself as a personal brand. I will guide you through my five acts of personal branding: Discover, Define, Design, Deploy and Deliver.

Part 3 is a reminder that there is no destination that you are striving to reach. Rather, you are always on a continuous journey of learning and evolution even when you reach the top of your organisation.

I'll then end with a 'How-to guide' on several diverse challenges young women face from how to ace a job interview to how to break the bias.

I believe that this holistic approach to professional and personal growth will help you go further, faster.

This book is not going to help you find the perfect match between your talents and the kind of work that will give you the deepest satisfaction at all levels. But I'm hoping that it will make you ask questions of yourself, evaluate where you are in life and think about the habits you want to adopt to move to a more fulfilling state on your journey.

You can read the book from start to finish or you can refer to the chapter outline and dip in and out as you please. My own life and work experience is the basis for this book and hence you'll find lots of personal stories which I hope will make it an interesting and relatable read.

My greatest wish is for you to take away ideas on mindset and tools to apply to your everyday working life. I hope it will make you better prepared to seize the wonderful career opportunities that are sure to come your way when you are well prepared.

Ready to start?

PART I

DEVELOP YOURSELF

Mind. Body. Soul

Why do you want to work? What purpose is work fulfilling in your life? What do you want to achieve with your work? What approach to work should you adopt?

I have observed that there are broadly three kinds of people when it comes to approaches to work and careers.

Some people just tick the boxes. They check in at 9 a.m. and check out at 5 p.m. or whatever the fixed hours of their workplace might be. I call them the cruisers. They are working to earn money. Their job may not be particularly meaningful to them. Their job funds their lifestyle, which may be more important to them. They are able to get by at their workplace by just cruising every day, doing the bare minimum to hold on to their jobs.

Others pour themselves into work and can't stop thinking about it, doing it or dreaming about it. They are the workaholics. Work is their religion. They will let nothing come in the way of their professional responsibilities. They routinely clock ten to twelve hours at the workplace if not more. They even work weekends.

And then there are those who value life outside of work but are stuck in dreadful jobs that require long hours. There is no escaping this drudgery for them. They must show up every day and grind through the day without much personal satisfaction. Often, they are disengaged and can bring down the energy of the work environment. I call them the miserables.

The Cruisers. The Workaholics. The Miserables.

We may identify with one of these types entirely. Or more likely, we have characteristics that fall into one or more of these types. In different jobs or at different stages in our career, we may naturally be inclined to one of these types more than the others.

The cruisers deprive themselves of a deeper connection with their life's purpose. The workaholics deprive themselves of leading richer lives. The miserables deprive themselves of daily motivation and inspiration from work by choosing unsuitable professions, which they may have ended up with due to parental pressure or financial reasons.

Is there another way? An approach that is soul-satisfying and not soul-crushing? Can we love what we do, be successful yet not sacrifice important aspects of being a human at the altar of work?

Yes, there is. It's a holistic approach to personal and professional development. This integrated approach helps us to protect our bodies, develop our minds and nurture our souls in the quest for achievement and success without sacrificing our physical, emotional or spiritual well-being.

Mind, body, soul – if you take care of these three, your career will take care of itself. Well, there will be a few other things you need to do, which we will discuss in Part 2 and 3 of this book. The foundation of a holistic Mind–Body–Soul approach is necessary to have a flourishing career and a life that matters.

1

Mind

LEARNING DOES NOT STOP when you graduate from high school or college. In fact, the worst career mistake you can make is to stop developing your mind.

Your mind is like a garden. You must nurture it. It is subtly reactive to every experience you have. Your thoughts are the seeds. You can either grow flowers or you can grow weeds.

Once you join the workplace, you may stop paying attention to the garden of your mind. How do you ensure that your mind doesn't become overgrown and unwieldy? How do you care for your garden in a manner that it grows into a beautiful space that gives you joy and satisfaction every day while feeding you the brainpower and creativity to fuel your life's calling? How do you give it the water, sunlight, nutrition and love it needs to flourish?

There are several practices that I have found extremely useful for cultivating my mind. In no particular order, they are reading, writing, journaling, silence, self-awareness, connecting the dots, mind management, developing 'range', resilience, goal orientation, feedback, achievement rather than activity and time management.

Engaging with Reading

You don't have to be born a reader, but if you want to be a leader, you must read. The most successful leaders are all voracious readers. They excel in both breadth and depth when it comes to reading. They can consume huge volumes of information in a matter of a few hours and be able to get to the nub of the ideas and bring new perspectives to the information. Getting to the crux of reams of information is Indra Nooyi's X-factor.

Indra, former Global CEO of PepsiCo, talks about this skill as the unique advantage she brings to the table.

My earliest memory of reading is my hunger for books when spending my summer holidays in Madurai with my grandmother and a few cousins who also came there for their vacation. I had hours to kill every day. The scorching sun ruled out outdoor activities for extended periods of time. My cousins were much older and saw me as a nuisance. It was the early 1980s and we had barely one channel on television – Doordarshan – and it used to broadcast the most unimaginative and boring shows. My safe space was with my books.

There was an old garage turned lending library in Chinna Chokkikulam, the tony neighbourhood in which my grandmother lived. I spent hours browsing the five hundred square feet of floor-to-ceiling shelves jam-packed with books, bringing back treasures to read and reread until it was time to return them. Jhelum, her palatial home, had a sprawling garden, with giant laburnum trees and an outdoor swing, which was one of my favourite reading nooks.

Enid Blyton was my top choice in my early years. St. Claire's, Famous Five, Secret Seven, Malory Towers – I devoured them all. This was followed by Nancy Drew and Hardy Boys and, eventually, Danielle Steele when I was in high school. As a teen, I eyed Mills & Boons secretly but feared my cousins' wrath, so I never dared to borrow one. I did read them surreptitiously at the library as much as I could! Archie's comics, Asterix and Tintin were also regular features in the stacks I borrowed. I was not reading at an advanced level at any stage, but I thoroughly loved reading and that was all that mattered. Or so I thought.

Back home with my parents during the school year, my mother nudged me to read the classics and to expand my repertoire, but reading took a back seat when I was neck deep in schoolwork, busy with extracurriculars like learning Carnatic music and Bharatanatyam and thoroughly enjoying sports like badminton and swimming. Television was also evolving in India, and by the early nineties, there was an explosion of TV channels. With over five hundred channels beaming into our homes, we were spoiled for choice. The junk box had become a huge source of distraction for youngsters. My parents had to set aside fixed hours for TV when they started to realise what a waste of time and energy it had become for me, leaving almost no hours in the school day for meaningful pursuits like reading.

It was only when I started preparing for the SATs in Grade 11 that I realised that my vocabulary was nowhere near the level required to ace the college preparatory test. I found the comprehension passages and analytical sections difficult. I was highly proficient with the Maths sections, but my Verbal scores were average. When this realisation dawned, I started studying vocabulary lists with great rigour, but I found there was only so much I could master in a year or so. On the other hand, had I spent my school years on advanced reading and learning, it would have greatly helped my vocabulary.

It was in college that I developed as a reader. My undergrad studies at Davidson College, a liberal arts college about thirty miles north of Charlotte, North Carolina, USA, transformed me from a basic reader to one who truly relished the written word. I read broadly with a ravenous appetite. It was at Davidson that I sowed the seeds that grew into a lifelong love of reading. While I had lots of reading to do for my classes, it was the reading list of my philosophy class on existentialism that truly upped the ante. We read Camus, Kierkegaard, Sartre and Simone de Beauvoir to name just a few. I was looking up words on every page, learning new words every day and being exposed to ideas I never knew existed. I was hooked. And I've never looked back.

Whenever I came home to Mumbai during the summer vacation, my first stop would be Shemaroo Library to borrow books and videos. At the end of the summer, my parents treated me to a mega shopping visit to Crossword, a trendy bookstore designed to be a nirvana for book lovers. That is when I discovered Indian writers writing in English, such as *English, August* by Upamanyu Chatterjee, *Half a Life* by V.S. Naipaul, *Unaccustomed Earth* by Jhumpa Lahiri and many more.

By my junior year in college, when it was clear that I was going to major in economics, I also started enjoying business books. *Odyssey: Pepsi to Apple* by John Sculley was the first business book that I truly enjoyed. The book, which details how Steve Jobs attracted John Sculley to Apple by asking him, 'Do you want to sell sugared water, or do you want to change the world?', totally captivated my imagination about the world of business. This line from the book has stayed with me as a reminder of the value of purpose in one's career.

Books were much cheaper to purchase in India than in the US. So my suitcases on the flight back to Charlotte were usually overweight from all the books I lugged back and, miraculously, found time to read while at college.

One of my all-time best reading years was when I was employed at my first job at Ogilvy Consulting, a division of Ogilvy & Mather Advertising, in Mumbai. R. Sridhar, my boss, had amassed the most incredible collection of books on advertising, marketing and branding. They were neatly stacked on shelves in his otherwise spartan office. The best part of all was that I had free and full access to all of Sridhar's books.

I gobbled up book after book as quickly as I could. Everything from *The Confessions of an Advertising Man* by David Ogilvy and *Disruption* by the good folks at TBWA (the famous ad agency that created the iconic 'Think Different' ads for Apple) to Harvard Business School journals and Fortune magazines. Sridhar travelled to other cities in India almost once a week and invariably returned with a pile of new books to devour. He was very fond of airport bookshops from which he picked up international best-sellers in business and non-fiction. This was a veritable treasure trove for me when I joined the workforce. My passion for the world of branding was sown here.

I had subconsciously picked up Sridhar's habit of buying books during trips. When I started working for Landor in San Francisco, the most exciting part of my business trips was spending time at airport bookstores choosing books for the trips. In-flight time was the perfect, uninterrupted time to lose myself in a book. I was not really tempted by the variety of content offered on the in-flight entertainment systems. I developed the habit of reading non-fiction and something relevant to my job on the morning flight and fiction on the flight back home. That way I felt less guilty about not working on flights. And that is how I grew as a reader.

What does reading do for me?

It makes me more knowledgeable. I can easily draw upon case histories of the past to bring more insight to a client conversation.

It keeps me up to date on the evolving world of business. Whether it is digital transformation or artificial intelligence, I can hold my own.

It gives me new ideas to execute, be it internal, to be tried with my team, or external, to be tried with clients.

It is a huge source of personal growth and development. I've become a better speaker, a better writer, a better leader and a better mentor – all thanks to books, especially all the non-fiction ones I've read.

It has made me a more interesting person who can effortlessly strike a rapport with anyone. I can easily start a conversation with anybody and establish a connection.

It has made me more creative. Fiction has increased my empathy, broadened my perspective and made me a more expansive thinker.

No matter where you are in your reading journey, how can you improve?

Commit a fixed time for reading every day. It can be as little as fifteen minutes and as much as you can devote. Warren Buffett spends eight hours a day reading. Don't go more than a few days without reading.

Don't read to impress. It should never be about what others are reading or what would make for a good cocktail party conversation.

Only read books that you enjoy. Ditch those that you don't. Life is too short. If an author is not using her craft to hold your attention, move on.

Keep books everywhere Keep them near your bedside, in the bathroom, scattered all over your house and even in your handbag. Time spent standing in line is time that could be devoted to reading.

Maintain a reading queue. When you read reviews, note down the names of authors and their books. Buy books whenever you can. Keep at least five more books with you than you are currently reading.

Be mindful of what goes in. Curate your reading list. Aim for a variety of genres, perspectives and topics. Diversity is key.

Write after you read. We lose so much of the information we take in. The depletion from our brains is tragic. Unless you write down your learnings and reflections, insights are going to vanish before you know it.

Embracing Silence

In the middle of the pandemic, I started seeing a therapist. Stuck in a Mumbai apartment with two teenage daughters and a husband who hated being cooped up at home, the domestic tensions were getting worse as the pandemic stretched out with no end in sight. Just when the girls sought less parental supervision, they got more of it. My husband and I couldn't help ourselves. We were constantly hovering around them when we weren't on work-related Zoom calls. We were getting on each other's nerves. At near breaking point, I sought professional help.

One of the first things my therapist asked me during our virtual session was how comfortable I was sitting in silence by myself and doing nothing.

'What do you mean doing nothing?' I asked quizzically. I'm always doing something every waking hour. Working or exercising or chatting or writing or having meals. Isn't that normal?

'Can you just sit by yourself and not engage in any activity?'

I certainly could not. The thought that I should had never occurred to me. I always had something to do. I just didn't know better.

This is when I learned about the practice of sitting in silence. It involves doing absolutely nothing but sitting with your thoughts, whatever they may be, not judging, just observing them come and go. It's about enjoying your own company.

My therapist asked me to sit comfortably on a chair with my feet firmly on the ground and look out in front of me. 'Just be,' she said.

It was incredibly difficult at first. A thousand thoughts raced through my mind. My to-do list kept popping up and random memories knocked at me. I was fidgety, constantly playing with my hair or scratching my face. I could barely sit for a few minutes without wanting to get up and do something. I didn't think it would take all my willpower to just do nothing.

As I began to cultivate this practice by sitting in silence for a few minutes more each day, I started enjoying this activity, if I may ironically call it one. I liked zoning out, being able to escape from the busyness and retreat to an imaginary place where nothing happened. I felt calmer, settled and far more at peace with myself.

What did silence do for me?

Silence helped me understand that racing from dusk to dawn is not sustainable. It takes a toll on my body and mind. It makes me less tolerant, less patient and a whole lot irritable.

I understood that even a moment of pause can offer a welcome change of pace while transitioning from one thing to another. A few such breaks punctuated throughout the day made it less hectic.

I was able to access a part of my consciousness that was otherwise out of bounds. It enabled me to think more clearly every day. It may have prevented some rash decisions in the heat of the moment.

It brought on more self-awareness and self-love. I felt less needy for validation, whether it were likes on my post on social media or praises from others for jobs well done.

It helped me erase 'crazy-busy' from my vocabulary. I just didn't like the sound of that phrase anymore. It made me sound like someone who careened out of control without any agency over her day. I was paranoid about being labelled as that person.

No matter where you are on your journey to more silence, how can you improve?

Schedule dates with yourself. This could be five-minute breaks, an hour of doing absolutely nothing or anything longer if you wish. The point is to do nothing on these dates and bring no one along – just have yourself for company. No other props like books, mobile phones, laptops or even pets.

Do not judge. As you enjoy silence, be careful that you do not start judging your thoughts. A lot will wash up during your moments of silence. Some of these thoughts may surprise you. Some may make you laugh. Others may make you cry. Let them pass. Observe and let go.

Make silence a part of your routine. Initially, I practised silence every day after my therapist first introduced it to me. Gradually, my schedule took over and I was inconsistent. Now I've worked moments of silence into my daily routine by pairing it with already established habits. Best-selling author James Clear calls this habit stacking. Choose a consistent time to be silent every day by pairing with a habit that is already a part of your routine. If you have tea every morning, for example, practise silence right before or after you've enjoyed your tea. Since the habit of drinking tea has already been wired into your routine, the chances of a new habit sticking will be that much more.

Silence is highly underrated. I hope you will give it a try to experience the transformational benefits it can bring you.

Dr Cicilia Chettiar, therapist, on the art of silence

The art of sitting quietly and doing nothing is currently almost non-existent. It should have been a normal practice, but it is being called an art, simply because staying still, without any stimulation is something that people seem to have lost the capacity for. Insane schedules – work or school, pressures and stresses, long commutes and deadlines have kept the brain in a hyperloop of endless activity. Sayings like the idle mind is the devil's workshop have made us misunderstand the importance of doing nothing. This is different from mindfulness, where one focuses single-mindedly on the task at hand. This is like taking your bra off after a long day of dressing up – just sit back and let things hang. While having an active, focused brain is essential for engaging with the world, developing the right skills and strategies to handle this engagement requires some quiet time. Thoughts may come and go as they need to. They could be anxious, depressed, angry, sad, happy, or neutral. But they all affect interoception – the sixth sense related to noticing signals from the body. One may notice hunger, thirst, or any other physical needs. But beyond that, the organs communicate through sensations. The English language is full of phrases that associate the mind with the body. For instance, we have a gut instinct, we shoulder our responsibilities, our heart aches for someone we love, our feet are rooted to the ground and so on. All these phrases reflect an emotional state explained through what's happening to an internal organ or a body part. If we fill up all our moments with noise, how will we listen to these messages? The messages are data that we must learn to process and utilise.

Sitting with yourself is not meditation. It helps if you can take regular deep breaths. Many confuse this as overthinking and fear it. It lets your thoughts disentangle from each other, make connections and associations based on its own intelligence without our focused interference, and most importantly, it allows you to listen to your body. The body is as intelligent as the brain. It's sharing information regarding feelings, emotions and instinct. Through interoception you will recognise where you have been rationalising a situation instead of recognising its unique meaning for you. The emotions that we may not pay attention to, because of our conditioning, are the guiding lights when we are faced with choices, decisions, and problem identification. Sitting still allows us to get in touch with them again, like releasing a tightly wrung towel. Memories are activated, the ability to be authentic is enhanced and consequently, the release of stress clears more space to process life authentically. Sitting still is not about being calm and peaceful and happy. It's about letting your brain do what it does best – process data without external interference. Merely having data is unhelpful, analysing it is fruitful. So be still. Let your brain do what it is meant to do.

Self-Awareness

One of the most efficient bosses I have had at Landor told me that self-awareness is a critical trait for advancing your career and being successful at the workplace. He had seen first-hand that many of our colleagues were not able to thrive because they were unaware of how they came across to others, which was getting in the way of their effectiveness. You may think of yourself as super smart, but others may see you as egoistic and non-collaborative. You may see yourself as being helpful, but your team may perceive you as a micromanager. Not knowing your strengths and/or not being fully in touch with how others perceive you are both career-limiting.

Self-awareness is a form of emotional intelligence that helps you understand your own emotions, behaviours, strengths, weaknesses and motivations and how these factors impact your relationships with your bosses, your peers, your juniors, your partners, your clients – essentially everyone in your ecosystem. It determines how effective you are as an employee in a particular organisational culture.

In a nutshell, self-awareness involves a keen understanding of the self as well as a keen perception of others. Having better self-awareness helps you be a better leader, make sound decisions and manage stress effectively.

As I have invested in improvement, I have learned three key things that improve self-awareness with regular practise.

Self-Reflection

Thinking about events that happened, how you reacted, the impact your actions had on others and the impact of others' actions on you, all of these help you understand yourself better. Journaling is a great way to engage in regular self-reflection. Ten minutes at the end of your work day is the best time and way to capture the day's impact on you.

Feedback

Feedback is indeed the breakfast of champions. One of my colleagues makes it a point to set up monthly chats with all her important colleagues to seek regular feedback. We asked her to conduct a session for all employees on what it means to embrace feedback and why it is critical to professional growth.

I have struggled with feedback, although I am aware of its importance. I am defensive by nature and don't like to be told I didn't do something properly. I like to think I am a very considerate person. I am not fond of being told that I made someone feel bad. But I learned that two people can respond differently to the same treatment. What style works for one may not work for another.

Additionally, when you are the big boss, people don't tell you the truth to your face. They only tell you what they think you want to hear. So, you must take extra trouble to seek feedback. It could be through formal mechanisms like a 360-degree feedback survey, a client satisfaction survey or the good old-fashioned way of simply having a frank conversation. Invest time to seek feedback – it will always be worth it.

Meditation

There is no better way to get in touch with the real you than by meditation, when you peel away all the extra layers to get to the core.

Meditation is not for everyone. It takes time and effort to get to a decent level but there are many apps you can download like Calm and Headspace that can give you a helping hand. I find that even ten minutes a day declutters my brain, providing me clarity of thought. The ideal length of time to meditate each day depends on your experience level and personal preferences. Experts say even 5–10 minutes a day is beneficial as a beginner and you can work your way up to 20–30 minutes, which is a decent level.

Self-awareness truly provides a good foundation for personal and professional development. It not only helps you understand yourself but also allows you to understand others better, leading to improved relationships and communication. These skills are invaluable as you progress in your career, making self-awareness a key factor in sustained and meaningful career growth.

Journaling

My earliest memory of writing a diary is from the third grade. I would cuddle up in my bed, ruminate about the day and share my most intimate thoughts with my diary. Every entry started with 'Dearest Diary' and ended with 'Very sleepy now, goodnight my Dearest Diary.' When I dug up the physical archives of all my childhood tchotchkes a few years ago at my parents' home, I was surprised to find scores of diaries in various sizes chronicling my growing years, right from primary school to twelfth grade. Clearly, this was a habit that had been ingrained in me, but I don't recall my parents ever asking me to maintain a diary. My best guess of how I picked up this habit is that I must have been imitating a favourite character from one of Enid Blyton's books.

Though I did not continue this habit when in college in the US (I switched to sending my parents long, handwritten letters chronicling my adventures), it did come in handy when I spent six months in France on a study abroad programme. I still have an exquisitely preserved journal detailing my entire semester in Tours, which I revisit often to cherish those memories and get some insight into the younger me.

Sadly, once I entered the world of work, there was no time for writing diaries. I was just trundling along from one year to another. If I could turn back the clock, I would maintain a diary of all my reflections and learnings from every day at work. What a rich repository of stories and life insights that would have been for me to tap into. It's never too late to start!

A few years ago, I came across a blog post by Benjamin Hardy (author of *Personality Isn't Permanent*) titled, 'How to write in your journal to improve yourself and achieve your goals', which gave me a new perspective on journaling. Writing in a diary at night felt too much like a childhood activity. Perhaps that's why I wasn't gravitating to it. Benjamin's testimony that daily journaling is the most important practice for personal growth and goal achievement gave me reason to take it up again. I learned from him that your journal is your most powerful resource for manifesting your dreams.

Picking up journaling as an adult, I switched from what was a nightly routine to a morning one. Journaling became the way to prime myself for the day's achievements. It was partly a to-do list and partly a list of priorities.

Brian Tracy's *Eat That Frog* advocates tackling your hardest task of the day first thing in the morning. The basic thesis of Tracy's book is to stop procrastinating. We can get easily distracted and busy with whatever grabs our attention in the moment. Being intentional about spending time on the hardest things that matter the most is key. Brian, an author and motivational speaker, was inspired by Mark Twain who once said, 'Eat a live frog first thing in the morning and nothing worse will happen to you the rest of the day.'

I like to spend five to ten minutes on my journal first thing in the morning. Sometimes I listen to a podcast on my way to work which motivates me in some aspect of leadership or management. I capture key insights in my journal and think about how to apply them in my day-to-day. I look at the day ahead in terms of scheduled meetings, I look at my running to-do list, I glance at my overall goals and then I focus on the one thing that has to be done that would make a difference. For example, if the task for the day is to write the outline for my brand transformation keynote presentation, I start with writing some thoughts about this. I may express gratitude for the opportunity, write down names of people I can speak to, who may help enrich content, or just jot down ideas related to the task ahead.

My mental preparation and handling of emotions for the day ahead happens during this journaling time. I think about what kind of physical and emotional energy would be expected from me given the goals. Is it going to be a walk in the park kind of day or more likely one with a few high-stakes meetings? Will any tough conversations need to be had or can I walk the floors high-fiving teammates and spreading cheer?

I also write in my journal when I am away from regular work, like on days off or on holidays. Very often I get some of my best ideas when I am disconnected from work. Having my journal handy and spending time to write down my thoughts has helped me immensely.

Very often I revisit old entries from my journal to see how I'm progressing. Are some big frogs escaping being gobbled up? Am I over-indexing the tactical and under-indexing the big hairy audacious goals, otherwise known as BHAGs in the corporate world? What else could I be doing to achieve my goals? My time journaling is my chance to have a conversation with myself about my work. I try not to be harsh or critical. It's important to be kind, to be understanding of why things may not be happening the way I want them to and then be productive about how to move ahead instead of beating myself up.

No matter where you are in your journaling journey, how can you get better?

Choose a journal. Choose a physical journal, not a digital one. The visceral feeling of connecting with your inner thoughts when putting pen to paper cannot be achieved by tapping a keyboard and capturing them digitally. Invest in a high-quality journal that looks good, feels good and motivates you to write every day. Choose a suitable writing instrument as well.

Schedule a regular time. The only way to ensure you will journal every day is to put in a recurring meeting in your calendar. Some people like to do it first thing when they wake up, others right before they start work. Some do a lunchtime slot and some prefer to journal at the end of the day. I favour mornings as I believe it sets the tone for your day.

Show up consistently. It's one thing for journaling to be on your schedule. It's another thing entirely to do it every day.

This is what separates the great from the good. Even if it's just a few sentences a day, show up and do the work. Consistency builds muscle. Consistency reaps rewards.

Use prompts. If you're struggling with what to journal about, use a journal with prompts or search online for the prompts that best work for you. Some examples include: What is my top long-term goal? Is there somebody with whom I can improve my relationship to help achieve my goals? What will it be worth for me to push past my fears? If I could be doing anything with my life right now, what could I be doing?

Be honest. Your journal is for you and you only. It's your private space. If you're worried about others reading your journal, make sure you store it safely. You should be brutally honest with yourself. What's the point if you're going to put a spin on the situation even when it's just to yourself? Your journal is where you freely share your feelings – your aspirations, your anxieties, your jealousies, your inadequacies, your burning desires – all in equal measure as and when you feel these emotions washing over you. Write as vividly about your dreams as you write about your demons and fears. Capture them all down, regularly.

Reflect on previous entries. It's a good idea to revisit your writings from time to time to see if you're progressing or not, to determine patterns in your behaviour and to reflect on your mistakes. One of my clients, the CEO of a large hotel company, once said to me that most of his success can be attributed to the time he has spent daily on writing about his day. He would focus on how his actions impacted others and how he could have done better in situations that did not go well or that had a negative impact on others.

When I speak about journaling, many youngsters ask me whether it is equally effective to journal using a digital app. My answer is an emphatic no. There are three simple reasons why I believe that journaling in a physical notebook is superior.

The first is that journaling allows you to shut out distractions and focus on your thoughts. It is an exercise in reflection. The disadvantage of firing up a Notes app on your phone, laptop or tablet is that you can easily get distracted by the notifications and before you know it, you've lost a few hours in doom-scrolling on the Internet. Even if you put your phone on airplane mode, the risk of getting distracted by something else is too high. Screening out all distractions is key to spending time with yourself and your thoughts.

The second reason I favour a physical notebook rather than a digital app for note-taking is the visceral connection between your subconscious mind and your pen. In my experience, the thoughts that flow when you put pen to paper have an emotional depth that are not always captured when you type on a laptop or a mobile phone. Julia Cameron's 'Morning Pages' in *The Artist's Way* builds on this insight that writing on paper allows you to access deep-seated feelings and emotions floating in the recesses of your mind.

The third reason why I prefer the physical medium is because I believe handwriting is still important in the digital age. It is such a core part of one's identity and so important to maintain. How often do any of us have opportunities to put pen to paper? Journaling is a great way to do so. Taking the time to write every day will hone your handwriting craft. Having beautiful handwriting can be an enhancer of one's identity.

Having made a case for journaling on paper, I don't want you to avoid journaling just because you may not favour this medium. Any journaling – even on digital apps – is better than no journaling!

Writing

I distinctly remember the first time I got formal feedback on my writing. It was for the first paper I had submitted for my English 101 class with Professor Zoran Kuzmanovich at Davidson College. We had to type and print out the assignment before turning it in. I had written about my first week in the United States as I had just arrived a few weeks prior. Despite a lot of my paper being marked up by the professor's red pen to correct my spelling and grammar mistakes, I was pleasantly surprised to read his encouraging comments at the end. He felt I had an easy, breezy and conversational style. He reminded me to spend more time on grammar and sentence structure while tying the whole piece together. I needed to connect the beginning and the ending as well as have a stronger thread running throughout the piece. My grade was a B+.

I didn't take any more English classes in college, but since I was studying at a liberal arts college, almost every subject except maths, a few economics classes and the language courses required me to be proficient at writing. I also had to learn a more formal style, which was different from my first English assignment.

The Elements of Style was my constant companion during my college years. My skills were most tested in the philosophy course. I not only had to understand complicated books by authors like Camus, Kirkegaard and Sartre, but I also had to write reflective essays on them as part of the assignments. I improved tremendously as a writer by the time I finished my four-year degree even though I majored in Economics and minored in Applied Mathematics. I had to take enough courses in the humanities to fulfil the core requirements which helped me hone my writing skills. It was only a few years later did I realise the importance of writing skills in leadership positions.

After undergrad, I had my next brush with writing in my second year at Landor when I was working in the San Francisco office. I sat at a desk not far from Larry Green, then our corporate web manager. He had full control over the content being published on our website. He saw that I was a reader, so Larry encouraged me to write. 'What should I write about?' I asked him, puzzled. Larry explained that brand consultants need to be thought leaders and that expressing your point of view by publishing opinion pieces on branding would be a good way to build credibility as a consultant.

I struggled for weeks on end on what to write. Perhaps I was too young and just didn't know enough to write with authority. Perhaps it was my inner critic that silenced me even before I began. Many aborted attempts and half-baked pieces are still saved on my hard drive.

It was when I moved back to India in 2006 that my writing finally took off. I realised very early on the importance of having your published work be easily found by anyone doing a basic search of your name on Google. I set out to proactively manage searches that came up when my name was Googled.

As the first employee of Landor in India, I had the massive responsibility of establishing the firm's reputation in the country, in addition to my own. Being a brand evangelist meant I had to talk about the benefits of branding for businesses at every opportunity I had. I grabbed every opportunity to write for publications and speak at conferences.

One year, I contributed a monthly article on branding for Campaign India. I had to submit a column every month. This kept the pressure on me to be disciplined about my output. Sometimes I left it to the last minute and struggled to put out a quality piece. Good writing takes time, and I learned that rushing through the process produced inferior output, which I would cringe about years later.

More recently, I started a weekly newsletter on personal growth and development. I choose one idea a week to bring it to life for my readers using personal examples. I also share links to places where they can learn more about that week's idea. Writing every week is not easy. It requires me to dedicate at least three to four hours just to write and edit the newsletter edition. The hard work has not been lost. I have managed to build a small community of newsletter subscribers who look forward to my writing every week. This has been wonderfully rewarding and motivates me to write more.

All these endeavours have made me not only a better writer but also a better thinker. Writing improves your thinking. When you can write about something in simple language, it means you have understood it.

What has writing done for me?

Writing has clarified my concepts. Every time I must write about something, it makes me work hard to understand it as fully as possible.

It has given me confidence as a creative professional. Being in the design industry, you can feel like an imposter if you are not a designer. Writing has given me the tools to feel like I am on equal footing with the creative stars in our industry.

It has opened myriad doors. One opportunity has led to another. Writing about how McDonald's conquered India led to me writing a foreword for a French author's book about being successful in the Indian luxury market.

Writing got me my own TV show. Well, writing established me as an authority on branding in India. When a producer at Bloomberg UTV was scouring the internet for a host for a possible show on branding, they found me! Hosting 'Beyond Logo', a TV show that ran on national TV for weeks, was one of the highlights of my career.

No matter where you are on your writing journey, how can you get better?

Believe in yourself. One of the greatest impediments to writing is our inner chatter. We're constantly judging ourselves. Saying that nothing we write will be good enough. We're not talented enough to be published. We don't have anything new or important to say. Fear of judgement holds us more back than anything else. Read *Big Magic* by Elizabeth Gilbert to overcome your anxieties and channel your voice to get published.

Read more. There is only one way to write better and that is to read more. Read everything you can get your hands on. Fiction and non-fiction. Blogs. Choose from a wide variety of genres. Pick up random articles on new topics that may not typically interest you. Observe how other writers use language and various techniques to create empathy, intrigue, interest and inspiration. What do they do to hook you? What type of writing disengages? As you read, make sure you are thinking about the craft of writing.

Write 'the ugly first draft'. Some of us struggle to go beyond the first sentence, the first para, the first page. We're judging already, fearful that it is not good enough. Whatever it is you are writing, just vomit it all out in the first go. Writers call it the shitty first draft. Keep writing without editing. Don't worry if it makes sense or not. The aim is to get it all out on paper. Once all is done, you can go to town with the editor's scissors to chop and shape to perfection.

Kill your darlings. Once you've done the draft, you must be willing to let go of pet phrases and sentences that may not serve the topic at hand. You can either delete them or save them all in one file as writer Celeste Ng does. This way you can always return to the graveyard when writing other pieces to give any dead sentences new life.

Write more. The best way to improve your writing is to write more. Write every day. Look for opportunities to be published. If not, start your own blog. LinkedIn encourages authors and is a good place to write regularly. The encouragement of your followers will give you the momentum you need to keep going. Dedicate a set number of minutes or hours every day to writing, depending on how integral it is to your job.

Other things to consider include joining a book club to read more, becoming part of a writing community (where writers help each other actively) or going on a Writers' Retreat or Residency to do focused and purposeful writing.

Writing is a meta skill in the 21st century. Marty Neumeier, a business innovator and best-selling author, is credited with coining the term 'meta skill' in his book *Metaskills: The Five Talents for the Future of Work*.

Think of a meta skill as a skill that can be applied to many different tasks and situations. Writing is a meta skill because it can be used to communicate, to learn, to solve problems and to create.

Master writing and you will go places in your career.

Management of Your Mind

Growing up as an only child, I never had much trouble managing my mind, which chiefly involved being able to concentrate and study when I had to. My parents didn't have to push me very much. I was naturally self-driven, which made me automatically disciplined about the hours I needed to put in. Luckily, my mind cooperated, falling into the rhythm. I was not distracted by too many things. My mind didn't get into a tizzy over teenage friendships or heartbreaks (though I had quite a few). I was also fortunate to have parents who were united in their outlook towards raising me. The domestic environment was stable. It didn't have any intense marital drama that many of my friends were subject to. My parents had their differences, but they never allowed it to impact my upbringing. I am also grateful that I didn't have to face sibling rivalry, abuse or depression in my childhood. I know how devastating each of those can be.

However, I did have to overcome other matters using the power of the mind in later years.

When I started travelling to the USA for my undergrad, I faced acute claustrophobia. As soon as I boarded the plane and the doors shut, I would have intense panic attacks. Sitting somewhere at the back of the plane in economy, all I would want to do is to get up and get out. My mind would be telling me I needed fresh air. That it wasn't a safe environment. 'Just get me the hell out of here' was my mindset. It was extremely tough in the first few years. It took me hours to calm myself. It usually involved confiding to my co-passenger about my claustrophobia and hoping they were kind, patient and tolerant enough to let me clutch their hand while I settled my nerves. I also used to ask for ice from the flight attendant, which would usually come well after take-off but helped make me less agitated about wanting to open the doors and jump off the plane.

How did I manage to travel back and forth for so many years despite being claustrophobic every time I got on a flight? My father came to the rescue. One summer he suggested that I chant *Vishnu Sahasranamam*, the thousand names of Lord Vishnu, which is a part of the Mahabharata. He even gave me his old copy of the English translation of this Sanskrit poem. What a brilliant suggestion and why had he not suggested it earlier? It worked wonders. I would start chanting the minute I got on the plane. The rhythm of the poem, the way my father had taught me to chant it and my intense focus helped me tide through till I was settled in for the long flight.

Isn't the mind a funny thing? One moment it's all worked up like a rough day on the seas and the next it's as calm and soothing as an ocean when there is no wind.

The thing to know is that you have power. You have the power to control your mind. To allow you to do the things you wish to do. To protect you from your fears and help you get ahead.

In the workplace, the fear I have had to deal with the most is public speaking. Despite years of doing it, I have still choked on a few big occasions. It's taken me every tool in my toolbox to succeed in those situations.

I have had a natural stage presence from a very early age. I distinctly remember a competition we had when I was in Queen

Mary's School. I must have been in the ninth or tenth grade. The entire school was assembled in the hall. We were waiting for a guest speaker who was really late, so our math teacher decided to help kill the time. He asked for volunteers to come on stage. He said we had to talk for two minutes without any pauses. We could choose any topic we wanted to speak on. I don't remember what I spoke about but I do remember I kept going without a pause. Two minutes felt like a very long time. And I won! I also participated in debates in QMS which honed my public speaking skills.

At Landor, I didn't have to do much public speaking in the first seven years of my career. I had to learn to be an engaging presenter when it came to client meetings, but the audience was never more than ten to twelve people.

When I moved back to India and set up Landor, one of the ways in which I set out to build the reputation of the agency was by making presentations at conferences.

One of the early opportunities I got was to speak along with Raymond Bickson (then the CEO of Taj Group, which is now known as Indian Hotels Company Ltd) and Ajoy Misra (then the senior vice president of sales and marketing at Taj Group) at the American Express Luxury Summit in Park City, Utah. Raymond, Ajoy and I had to talk about the brand transformation the Taj Hotels enabled by their new brand architecture strategy recommended by Landor.

Imagine my first public speaking opportunity was at such a high-powered international conference along with my clients who were industry captains. The Amex Luxury Summit usually attracted the top marketers for the luxury industry in the US. It was a huge honour that they had invited an Indian brand to present a keynote at this conference.

Ajoy and I had prepared the presentation. We had a few rehearsals in Bombay before we left for the US. I travelled with Ajoy and thought we would practise on the flight or in the lounge in London while waiting for our flight to Newark and then onwards to Park City. Unfortunately, Ajoy – as experienced as he was – had no interest in rehearsals on the journey. I tried to go over my bits of the presentation a few times, but my nerves got to me. I left it aside hoping and praying to not crash the presentation, which was in a few days.

Once we got to Park City, I spent every waking hour practising. I cajoled Ajoy and Raymond to have a few more practice sessions with me though they probably didn't need it.

I remember how dry my mouth was just as I was to go on stage to continue the presentation after Raymond had set up the context. When I got on, the lights blinded me. I could barely see the audience, which was around two hundred fifty people, eager to learn about how an Indian luxury hospitality company was thinking about its brand strategy.

I paused for ten seconds, took a deep breath and then started. I had a slightly nervous, shaky start but I got more confident with every sentence as I found my footing on stage and reminded myself how important it was that I do well for my client.

I didn't wreck the presentation as I had imagined I would. It was the opposite. I was insightful and charismatic, or so I was told. I got compliments from my co-speakers as well as many in the audience who I had a chance to interact with during the tea break. They had several fascinating questions based on what I had shared.

How did I overcome this fear and manage not to be paralysed on stage?

I knew the content cold. I had practised it a thousand times over. I was comfortable with Raymond and Ajoy. They wanted me to succeed, which was a huge motivator. And then perhaps everything else kicked in – the years of client presentations and, of course, the adrenaline.

There were two more occasions when high-powered situations got the better of me and I had to manage my mind to swing a successful outcome.

Several years ago, I was invited to be a keynote speaker at a Tech Mahindra conference in Hyderabad for their Top 200 executives from around the world. By then I had enough public speaking opportunities to hone my skills, but this event got the better of me. Maybe it was the seniority of the audience. Maybe I felt that being a B2B company, they would not really be interested in how brands can help them.

I was a nervous wreck for the two weeks leading up to the event. Initially, I was stressing so hard on the content that I could not focus on the delivery. Then when I started practising,

I would second guess the content flow and want to rewrite it all over again. This kept me in a state of constant paranoia.

On the day of the event, Ronnie Screwvala was slated to speak before me. I'm doomed, I thought to myself. He's a hard act to follow. I paced up and down backstage, my stomach churning. I took deep breaths when possible. I had to go to the washroom a few times. I had to silence the incessant chatter in my mind that was telling me that I was going to fail. I visualised myself on stage in Park City at the Amex Summit and reminded myself that I could do it. I recalled the wonderful compliments I got and reassured myself that I knew what I was talking about.

When it was time to get on stage and begin with my presentation, it was just fine. I could see the audience. Some of their nodding heads gave me the positive reinforcement I needed and kept me going. Here again, muscle memory kicked in and my adrenaline tided me over. I even got a resounding applause at the end!

There is one more story I want to tell you about how I managed my mind to craft and deliver an impactful presentation to a global audience. This was in 2022 at the Cannes Lions Festival of Creativity, which takes place annually in the south of France. I was a part of the Landor delegation. Our parent company WPP was sponsoring a client conclave at Cannes. They had invited me to be one of the fresh voices from the company who would present at Ignite, an inspiring talk series held every day at WPP Beach on the Croisette in Cannes.

Despite being an experienced brand consultant, the very thought of having something super insightful to say to the top marketers in the world from the likes of Unilever, Meta and Google gave me the jitters. Besides, the Ignite format was very punishing – you are only allowed fifteen slides. Once started, each slide would automatically move to the next after fifteen seconds. You had no control over the pace of the presentation. The only saving grace was that you could speak on whatever topic you thought might interest the audience, but it couldn't be a sales pitch for your company.

The whole act of conceptualising my Ignite talk, crafting the overarching narrative, writing the script precisely (so my talking points for each slide did not exceed fifteen seconds), preparing the accompanying visuals to look stunning and then practising repeatedly was excruciatingly difficult. I regretted having signed up. This was way tougher than I had ever imagined. Plus, our CEO had told me she wanted my talk to be the most memorable. Talk about performance pressure. To make matters even more stressful for me, I knew that our entire Landor delegation at Cannes would be in the front row rooting for me, as would some very senior people from WPP. This could be career-defining or career-destroying. The choice was mine.

Looking back, having participated in Ignite was one of the best experiences of my professional life. It taught me the value of telling a story well, being economical with your words and being in perfect rhythm with your props.

I know these aren't the last occasions in which I have needed to control my mind. I'm sure to encounter more situations. But these stories serve as important reminders that I can and I will overcome them every time.

No matter where you are in your mind management journey, how can you get better?

Don't skimp on doing the work. The fear your mind encounters can be sufficiently managed with enough preparation. I recorded myself presenting and listened to it ad nauseam in the last few days leading up to my session.

Believe in yourself. You must believe you will overcome your fear. Constantly chatting with your mind like you would a companion is important. Distance yourself. Give yourself a gentle talking-to if things are getting out of control. Bring yourself back to even keel.

Take deep breaths. Every time your heart starts to race, you begin to panic, and the heat rises in your body, close your eyes, count to ten, and breathe in and breathe out deeply. It's unbelievable how much more in control you will be halfway through. By the time you reach ten, the fear will have vaporised. Almost.

Time Management

One of the questions that I get asked a lot is how I manage to do so many things – in other words, people are seeking as much guidance as they possibly can on the topic of time management.

There's so much to do but so little time.

I hear this phrase often, but I don't see it as a challenge. I have managed to find the time for the things I must get done and for the things that I love to do.

How do I manage to find a rhythm and pace to my day?

The seeds of good time management were sown in my childhood. Ours was a household that was up at the crack of dawn, typically no later than 5:30 a.m. Both my parents would be awake and getting started with their day. My father is a Vedic scholar and very religious. I grew up listening to him chanting *Divyaprabhandam* and *Vishnu Sahasranamam* in the mornings. My mother is a social worker and an avid reader. I used to see her devouring the morning papers while sipping her piping hot tea in *davara* tumblers. Maybe she is the one I picked up my tea habit from.

While my parents were busy with their morning routines, I used the early morning hours before school to study. You can't help but focus and concentrate when the environment is reverberating with the soothing sounds of chanting. After our morning rituals, we would start getting ready for school and work. By 8 a.m., all of us were out the door.

What time did I go to bed if I was waking up by 5 a.m., people ask me. In my childhood and up to college, it was no later than 9 p.m. Sometimes I would even go to bed at 8:30 p.m. if it had been a long day. It helped that my parents were not big TV watchers, did not go out much for a meal (maybe once in a few months at most and usually for lunch) and did not host dinner parties (except the occasional corporate party my father had to host a few times a year). Eighteen years of following the circadian rhythm with this kind of discipline does get wired into your operating system.

I must say though that when I was in college in the US for four years, this pattern was put to a severe test. No college student goes to bed that early. You would get skewered by your friends and would have no social standing if you did that. While in college, I had to adjust my schedule to a 7 a.m. wake-up to sleep-at-midnight schedule.

Thankfully, I was able to return to my childhood habits when in business school and then subsequently when I started in the world of work. I was at the SP Jain Institute of Management and Research in Andheri, a Western Suburb of Mumbai. I had decided to stay at home in Churchgate with my parents and commute. Even though classes would begin at 8:30 a.m. sharp, I would usually be the first one to arrive despite having a one-hour commute on the Churchgate–Andheri fast train in the mornings. Even when we did go out at night and stay out till midnight or even 1 a.m., I was awake by 6 a.m.

I distinctly remember my classmates commending me for always being on time despite living the farthest from our campus. Similarly, when I started my career at Landor in San Francisco, I had a one-hour drive to work every morning from Redwood City, where my husband and I had found a house to rent when we first moved to Silicon Valley. While driving to work in the mornings, up Interstate 280, the famous scenic highway between San Jose and San Francisco, I used to listen to *Vishnu Sahasranamam* in the car. I had no trouble waking up, getting ready and starting my drive by 7:30 a.m. I was usually one of the first to show up every morning at Landor's iconic former headquarters at 1001 Front Street, San Francisco.

It truly is amazing how habits embedded in childhood follow you through life. I never thought chanting would have a place in my life. I'm not religious at all but the peace that chanting gave me was like no other. I automatically gravitated to making it a part of my morning drive without much effort. Maybe in my mind it was inexplicably paired with waking up early. It certainly put me in a great state of mind by the time I reached the office and fired up my laptop, ready for the tasks of the day ahead.

The early-to-bed and early-to-rise habit was particularly helpful when I gave birth to my daughters. Anyone who has been a parent and who does not delegate bedtime and wake-up time with your children, especially in their early years, knows how valuable it is to be able to follow your babies to bed and wake up early with them. A lot of the deep bonding happens in these hours!

Going to bed early and waking up early is the foundation of my time management system. When you get a good night's sleep and can rise early, it naturally creates the right mindset and rhythm for the day. You are less prone to waking up in a bad mood and rushing through your morning routine, which can have a cascading effect on the rest of your day. Getting annoyed over the littlest of things, irritability with co-workers, afternoon slumps, making poor food choices – these are all manifestations of poor sleeping habits.

My time management system became more rigorous after I read Robin Sharma's *5 AM Club*. Robin's book showed me that it is not just about waking up early. How you spend those first few hours is critical. Do it right and it can have a transformational effect on your productivity and creativity, giving you a gargantuan competitive advantage.

When I audited my first hour of the day, I realised that I was whiling it away. I was diving into the news, getting distracted by social media and looking at my emails. All of these activities were getting me into the wrong frame of mind before a long workday ahead. Waking up early is only half the job. Making the waking hours meaningful is the other half, arguably the more important one.

Robin advocates three twenty-minute segments for your first hour in the morning. Movement. Meditation. Mind enrichment.

The first twenty minutes are dedicated to getting your body moving. Ideally, you would go outdoors for a twenty-minute walk or run. Movement fires up the cells in your body and gives you the momentum you need in the morning.

The next twenty minutes are dedicated to meditation and reflection. Ideally, you would sit cross legged on a mat on the floor and close your eyes. What physical exercise is to the body, meditation is to the mind. It clears your brain clogged with toxins such as cytokines, an inflammatory chemical created by stress, and gives you the clarity you need to conquer your day.

The final twenty minutes are for mind enrichment. Read a book, listen to a podcast, watch an inspirational video. Engage your mind in something which enriches your brain. Filling your mind with stimulus every day makes it a fertile ground for creativity to flourish.

After reading Robin's book, I practised the method diligently for four to five months. I then loosely adapted it to create my perfect mornings. The philosophy is intact, but the activities and time spent on each are different.

So what does my perfect morning look like?

5:30 a.m.	Wake-up
5:40–5:45 a.m.	Deep Breathing
5:45–6:00 a.m.	My Morning Pages (3 pages in my diary about anything whatsoever – just emptying the monkey mind of all the thoughts it is holding when I wake up.)
6:00–7:15 a.m.	Workout (Mon/Wed/Fri – weight training and cardio) (Tue/Thu – yoga) (Sat – tennis) (Sun – rest day)
7:15–8:00 a.m.	Get ready for work.
8:00–8:30 a.m.	Some meditation + listen to a podcast in the car on the way to work

This has become an integral part of my everyday routine. Starting on this note with movement, meditation and mind enrichment gives me the necessary energy, clarity and inspiration for the day ahead.

What about the day at work? Should it be filled with endless meetings and becoming a slave to email?

I used to arrive at work, open my laptop and get started on emails right away. With Outlook always on and my phone by my side, I was in a constant state of distraction. I could barely focus on an email response when a client's text would arrive screaming for my immediate attention. I might be typing a response when a colleague would stop by my desk and ask about a client deliverable that was due later that day. This constant shifting of tasks takes a heavy cognitive toll. This is what creates exhaustion by the end of the day.

One of my former senior colleagues, Mike Staniford, an executive creative director, taught me about time blocking. You must schedule blocks of time in your daily calendar for deep, focused work, otherwise you will not produce any work at work! Being a knowledge worker in the field of creativity, your measure of value is in the work that you and your team produce. Set aside this kind of time to do the work rather than just floating through the day attending meetings and answering emails. It's not easy in a culture of excessive meetings and email communications, but if you don't treat at least part of your time as sacred, it will surely get hijacked.

Another habit that helps (especially for working mothers) is to keep work and home separate. When at work, be fully present at work. When you come home, leave your work behind.

Keeping work and home separate requires some trade-offs. I had to learn to be fiendishly focused to get the tasks done. In the early years, it wasn't always easy. I had to squeeze in work at home either early in the morning or late at night – usually the former – to write presentations, create thought leadership pieces and do extra reading for work. As I rose up, I tried to do as much work during office hours as possible. Sometimes, I still need to dedicate part of my weekends to get some important work done but that's par for the course for me. If you want to be recognised as an expert in your field, you must put in those extra hours to create that edge for yourself. But the principles of time management as outlined above still guide me to prevent me from becoming a workaholic and caring about work above everything else. Arguably, this separation has become very difficult for most of us to manage post-Covid-19, with the lines between work and home becoming extremely blurry.

What about time for other pursuits? Mine are reading, content creation, cooking and sports to name a few. How did I manage to squeeze these in?

Reading is an easy one. I read sometimes in the morning, always on plane rides and often for half an hour to an hour before going to bed. Cooking was mostly done on the weekends, when I had a lot more time on my hands to plan meals, get the shopping done and cook without any pressure. I do content creation on the fly whenever I have some free time. It could be when my kids are studying and I need to sit with them but not teach them. For this as well, weekends afford me a lot of time. It helps that I'm not addicted to Netflix.

What has time management done for me?

It has helped me consistently make time for the things that would help me succeed at work.

It has given me more time for my family and other pursuits outside of work.

It has allowed me to pace myself, so I don't feel overworked or burnt out.

It has given me purpose and meaning. I never feel I am whiling away my time even when my days and weekends are punctuated with time for rest and relaxation.

No matter where you are on your time management journey, from novice to expert, how can you get better?

Start with a time audit. For two weeks (no more and no less), keep a diary in which you note down every way in which you spend your time, from the moment you wake up to the time you go to bed. This can be very tedious, but what you find about your habits after two weeks will be well worth the trouble. Be brutally honest. Even if you must write down that you spent 95 minutes one Thursday evening mindlessly watching reels on Instagram, write it down. Don't judge yourself in the two weeks of auditing your time.

Once you have tracked your activities fastidiously for two weeks, take a step back and analyse the patterns. Are you spending your days in the way you wish to spend them? Which activities are taking up most of your time? Which activities do you barely spend any time on? For example, perhaps you think you spend a lot of time with your toddler, but the tracker shows barely a few hours a day. On the other hand, your social media average per day is four. Maybe you think you are reading every night before bed, but your tracker shows you manage some reading hardly a few nights a week. Or it registers too many hours spent responding to emails. What else shows up? Are you finding time for the things that you enjoy? Are you doing things that you should be delegating to others? How do you feel about how you've spent your time in the last two weeks?

Draw the arc of your day. The arc of your day becomes the arc of your life. If you don't find time for something in a day, it's unlikely to show up in your life as an important activity.

Think about segments, for example, family, work, exercise, hobbies, friends, spirituality. Plot your day to include time for all the segments. You don't have to be tied to your schedule, but it starts to make you conscious and gives you intentionality on how you will spend your day.

Wean yourself off time-wasters. You'll never have time for everything in life. You must give up some things to make more time for others. People ask me how I read so much. What they don't see is that I barely watch TV. Rather than reading the news on your phone or scrolling through your social media feeds when you're waiting somewhere and have some time to kill, take a mental break. Don't indulge in an activity from which you find it hard to disentangle.

Block time for meaningful pursuits. Most people looking for more time are doing so to achieve something. Want to write a book? Write 100 words a day. Want to get better at playing the guitar? Practise for an hour every day. Want to stay healthy and fit? Dedicate 30 minutes to exercise daily. Do you remember being taught the concept of compound interest in your eighth-grade Maths class? A little bit every day adds up to a lot by the end of the year. James Clear who wrote the bestseller *Atomic Habits* likes to call this 'the power of tiny gains.' One per cent improvement every day leads to being 37 per cent better at the end of the year. This can only happen by doing the work and improving day in and day out.

Banish 'crazy busy' from your vocabulary. Have you noticed how people love to boast that they are crazy busy? How much are they getting done? Doesn't matter but the perception of being busy not only leads them to feel overwhelmed and exhausted but also makes them feel there is no time. Our former global CEO Jane Geraghty cautioned us not to confuse activity with achievement. This couldn't ring truer in the world of work. Everyone is busy, but what do they have to show for it? Very often, not much. I have found that once I stopped telling people how busy I was, I not only felt better and less overworked but also found time to do the things I wanted. It's a very subtle mindset shift but a powerful one.

Connecting the Dots

I first read about this concept when Steve Jobs referenced it in one of his college graduation speeches where he was the convocation speaker. I was mesmerised by his stories of connecting the dots, but I couldn't quite understand what it meant.

The penny dropped for me after reading Todd Henry's *The Accidental Creative*. Todd calls himself an arms dealer for creative professionals. In this book that I have recommended to people more often than any other, we learn about practices and tools that we must deploy to be 'creative at a moment's notice.' It flies against the face of popular imagination that creatives have unstructured days and that they whip out creativity with ease. You learn that the best creatives are the most structured. They have processes and a rhythm to their days that allows their creativity to flourish. They have the ability to 'connect the dots.'

What does it mean? It's the ability to see connections between seemingly disparate pieces of information, to pull back and see the forest for the trees, to be able to synthesise, not just analyse, the information.

As knowledge workers, our value is determined by the quality of our thinking. We call it the Big Idea in advertising and marketing. Being able to connect the dots gives you the ability to be an ace problem solver – to rise above ordinary solutions, to develop original ideas and to put together thoughts in hitherto unimagined ways.

What has being able to 'connect the dots' done for me?

It has enabled me to reflect on my childhood to become more self-aware. I'm better able to understand why I am the way I am or why I operate in a certain way. It has given me the ability to appreciate my strengths and be more patient with the things I am not able to do well. I can connect the dots back to experiences in my childhood which may have been the springboard for my behaviours and preferences today.

It has made me a more prolific idea generator. I can easily contribute to brainstorming sessions. I'm usually the one with the highest quantity of ideas shared.

It has made the content I develop richer. I put together an online master course on Brand Building for a cohort of twenty-five women from leap.club in 2021 which was hugely appreciated based on the feedback. My course on personal branding is popular for the same reason. Participants say that I have brought them so many different ideas and woven them together in a compelling way.

No matter where you are on your 'connecting the dots' journey, how can you get better?

Fill your mind with diverse stimuli. What goes in comes out. An important element of being able to connect the dots is to have many dots in your mind in the first place to enable connections to happen. Enable this for yourself by taking in diverse stimuli for your brain. Read more, read different genres. Pick up magazines you wouldn't normally read. Every bit of information you consume becomes a dot that holds the possibility of a brilliant connection. Watch movies. Go to museums. Listen to different genres of music. Have conversations with different types of people. Travel the world. Pick up new hobbies.

In other words, experience life as richly as you possibly can. This is the finest way to fill your mind with dots. Our former global chief creative officer, Peter Knapp, used to remind us that we are in the best profession in the world as creative professionals. Who else gets paid to read a book, watch a movie or go to the museum? It works because your next brilliant insight or breakthrough idea might just come from one of those experiences.

Reflect on what you've experienced. As you fill your mind with diverse stimuli, you should also take the time to reflect on the things you are putting in. Journaling (which I wrote about earlier) is a good way to ensure that you are writing down your experiences. After you read an article or finish a book, write about what you learned. Do the same for everything else you experience, whether that inspires you or not. Some people journal at the end of the work day, others at night. Some start the morning with journaling. Do what makes most sense for you but don't neglect reflecting on the stimuli you are putting into your mind. Without this crucial step, the chance of your dots colliding into magical ideas are much less.

Take time to 'marinate'. The most important step of being able to connect the dots is this one: call it silence, meditation or just being in the present. If you are always on and busy with an activity, there will be very few chances for the magical process of connecting the dots to work in your brain. For that, you need to give it regular rest periods. Go for a walk outdoors without your phone and earbuds or headphones. Take a massage. Sit silently for an extended period. Do whatever helps you best to still your mind, to be present. Don't worry about the marination of dots that is happening in your brain. It is a wonderful process that is hard to explain. You must trust that it is happening.

One example of me being able to connect the dots was when I was invited to give a TedX talk at BD Somani International School a few years ago. The event was going to be attended by students and their parents. I decided to talk about the importance of vulnerability in how you live your life. I felt this topic would resonate with both audiences. When it came time to write the speech, I had to focus my thoughts and think of the narrative arc of my presentation. As I thought through incidents in my life at my most vulnerabe moments, it occurred to me that vulnerability had been a common thread in three areas: my work (brand and design), how I approach creativity and how I approach leadership. It was only by looking back – as Steve Jobs said – was I able to connect the dots and create a narrative for my TedX talk.

That's it. Keep doing this and you will notice that your ability to think more expansively, produce higher quality ideas and join the dots will vastly improve.

Pavithra Dikshit, Design Director, Landor, on connecting the dots

As a creative person, I have interests that are dime a dozen. With the pursuit of being inspired and stimulating my senses, I tend to go down rabbit holes of learning, conversation and research. Some I make into hobbies, some tend to become habits, some just wander in my mind in a space withheld for the future.

I have no way to know how I will join the dots or if they will ever join or are these the correct dots to pursue. But I don't really worry in the present about how something will be useful in the future. It eventually adds up. That is how the universe works. A couple of months ago, at Late at Tate's in London, I was visiting to see art but ended up discovering new music! And that has inspired a whole new range of thinking for a project I am presently on. On another occasion, a Henri Matisse exhibit at the MoMA in New York in 2014 inspired a typeface I designed in 2023. Serendipity? Maybe.

I never know how and when these myriad interests will align or when the dots will join. However I do know that the continuous inquiry into different interests impacts and influences my thinking and practice. Input = Output. Aptly summarised by this quote in the book *Bon Voyage* that I read at OFR, Paris: What makes me, 'me'? Not my ideas, not my body, not my skills, but my recipe of the world.

And like everything else, recipes evolve. There is no real perfect recipe. And yet, like salt, the common ingredient for everything I do is curiosity.

Building Resilience

I learned the meaning of resilience at the workplace from the very week I joined Landor. It was January 2001. The American economy was in shambles. There had been massive overheating from the irrational exuberance of the dotcom boom. A stock market crash was imminent. Consulting firms like ours had already picked up the softness that we experienced in the form of reduced demand for our branding and design services.

The management team at Landor's San Francisco studio had decided to lay off a significant number of employees. My name was on the initial list of those whose employment was to be terminated but had subsequently been taken off. My hiring manager had managed to convince the decision makers that I had skills that would be useful to the company in the long term. He took a bet on me that saved my job. I will be forever grateful because his faith in me has propelled me for over twenty-four years across continents with the same company.

On the day after the layoffs, predictably, the environment in the office was very glum, on top of an already gloomy and cold San Francisco winter day. Those of us who were left behind didn't have much work to do. It remained the same for several days after that first gloomy day. I would go to work, fire up my laptop, surf the web, chat with colleagues, eat lunch, fix myself many coffees and then go home early. I felt helpless and tried not to feel anxious. I was too low in the pecking order to be stressed about turning the company around. I just tried to stay under the radar and avoid looking obviously jobless.

One day, a senior business development director of the firm came by my desk while he was walking around. He was from another department, one I didn't usually interact with. I could have just exchanged niceties, but I decided to talk to him and ask how I could help. That one gesture began to turn things around for me. I started doing research on companies, building presentations and being roped in for pitches and proposals. This allowed me to interact with new people in our firm outside of my team. Being busy and having a purpose of aiding the new business team allowed me to embrace each day with anticipation instead of dread. I took each day as it came. I didn't focus on being fearful about what the future had in store (and if there was a possibility of me being laid off), but I focused on what I could contribute each day. It took seven months, but things did get positively better.

There was another incident when I was working in our London studio. I was taken off a project without being given proper reasons as to why I could no longer be a part of the team. This hit my self-confidence in ways I had not anticipated. I was ready to quit the firm. I would cry every day wondering what I had done so wrong.

For weeks I couldn't face others in the office. I felt so humiliated. My husband watched me every day. It's not his personality to cry over spilt milk and he hated watching me beat myself up about it, One day he pulled me aside and gave me a stern no-nonsense talking down. He said I might not agree with the decision that was taken. I may no longer even like the people who had made the decision, but I had to act mature, respect the decision, leave it aside and get on with things. I didn't like what he said but I followed his instructions. I pulled myself together and got on my A game from the next day. It didn't feel great inside, but I persisted with an optimistic approach. I threw myself into other projects. I made new friends. And after a few weeks, I felt better about myself. It still hurt when I saw the team I was booted off when they were busy with their work, but I learned to numb the pain.

In the course of my career, I have been on teams that have lost big pitches, but life went on. I have been at the receiving end of angry client calls, but life went on. I have had employees complain bitterly about this or that, but life went on. I have had talented employees who quit, and it seemed like the world would come crashing down, but life went on. I called in sick on some days when I could not get out of bed and thought the business would come to a standstill, but life went on.

Life goes on. This is what I have learned about resilience. We must go with the flow. When we are down, we must find a way to pick ourselves up. Wake up and show up. Showing up is half the work done. Do that and very often the rest will follow. We must also not take things to heart by focusing on the past. Forgive and forget. Easier said than done but that is the only way to release the pain and give yourself energy for the present. Keep doing this when you have setbacks, and you will build resilience. You will be able to soldier on despite difficult circumstances.

Sometimes you may not be able to pull yourself out of a situation. Consult with family and friends. Or get professional help in the form of counselling or therapy. I have seen some colleagues who desperately need help, but they don't want to admit they may have a problem that needs fixing. Don't fail to recognise when your emotional health is off and when a proper diagnosis and treatment is required.

More important, recognise that your highs won't last forever. Sometimes we are on such a trip of achievement and success that we forget what goes up does come down. We won't always be in a permanent state of high. Staying grounded and not getting carried away by the success is a part of preparing yourself to be resilient. Success is temporary. It might well come crashing down at a moment's notice. Be mindful of that as you go about when times are good. This will build your resilience for when things fall apart, as they inevitably do.

Goal Orientation

I have a confession. I was not a supremely goal-oriented person. Can you be successful without having clear goals? This is what I keep thinking about. The environment and processes at work make sure that you achieve clear goals collectively and individually. So how have I survived so many years in the corporate world without a proper system for regularly exceeding my goals? Could I have been more successful much faster had I been maniacal about goals? Perhaps.

To be clear, on the work front, I always knew directionally what I wanted to achieve, and I instinctively organised my day to ensure that my tasks would help us meet and exceed expectations as a team. I was clear with my leadership team what the expectations were and the areas in which we needed to excel. We didn't write down our goals, break them down into achievable bits and gradually make progress. It was a more loose and organic process of moving towards a destination.

On the personal front, I was driven by the idea of being the global CEO of a creative agency one day. This meant I had to consciously build my personal brand and put myself out there. I spent time building my website, writing my newsletter and being active on LinkedIn and Instagram. I signed up for courses that would help me be a better leader. I was always seeking things that could help in this pursuit.

A goal is nothing but a dream with a deadline. I certainly had dreams, but I was not applying enough urgency to realise them. This is where being much more rigorous with a system to achieve goals can come in handy.

I started researching more on the best way to achieve goals faster. I spoke to my mentors and others who have achieved phenomenal goals.

What have I learned and now put into action?

Write your goals down. Preferably, write them down in a place where you can see them every day. Research shows that people who write down their goals are more effective in achieving them. Some people swear by vision boards, which can be hugely motivating. A vision board is a collage of images representing your dreams. It helps you think years ahead. Your goals can be segregated by type or lumped together depending on what works for you. There can be so many types of goals – personal goals, professional goals, health goals, financial goals, family goals and so on! By writing them down and seeing them every day you are subconsciously giving direction to the way you choose to spend your time.

Make your goals time bound. By when do you want to achieve them? This is important because it creates the necessary motivation for action.

Break down your goals. Dreams can be abstract and big by nature. Breaking it down is helpful to see what you need to do today to work towards the dream. Think of a ladder with the dream at the top. What might you need to accomplish to get to the top?

Keep track. Write down progress. Keep an eye on things that are tripping you up. Remove obstacles in the way. Constantly work towards your goals.

Don't be too harsh on yourself if you haven't made progress for weeks. Just get back into action and then keep at it. It may be a good idea to share your goals with family or friends or anyone else who cares enough to ask about your progress and who will hold you accountable. I love what Tony Robbins says, 'Setting goals is the first step in turning the invisible into the visible.'

Achievement, Not Activity

The one big watch-out as you achieve your goals is not to confuse achievement and activity. They are not the same thing. A lot of people think that if you are super busy running around from meeting to meeting, then you must be getting a lot done. This could not be further from the truth. Like I referenced earlier, you can't confuse activity with achievement. Bustling around with an air of importance does not necessarily translate into accomplishment of goals.

One of the keys to success at the workplace, which I discussed in the earlier section, is to have clearly articulated goals which you work towards in a focused manner with relentless drive. Without focus, it is very easy to fall into the abyss of emails and meetings, which give you the false notion of having a lot to do. If your boss has not clearly defined the goals for you, define them yourself. Don't have a laundry list. Draw up a list of not more than three to five big things you must succeed at to add value to the business in your role. You must work backwards. What goal is the business trying to achieve? What must your team contribute? And hence what does that translate into when it comes to your contribution? Thinking this way allows you to connect more deeply with the purpose of the organisation. This will improve your motivation and drive every day.

The One Thing by Gary Keller and Jay Papasan advocates that by constantly drilling down to the one task that will move you close to your goals, you can make remarkable progress every day. This ensures that you are relentlessly focused on the outcomes and achievements, not just on the activities.

Think about the one most important thing to be accomplished each day and get it done before distractions get to you. Can you get the most difficult task on your list completed first thing in the morning? Accomplishing that gives you a sense of achievement that carries through in your positive attitude the rest of the day. For me, I do my writing first thing in the mornings whether it is writing an article, storyboarding a presentation or working towards my book.

The most important skill you must master to accomplish your goals is to stave off distractions. The alluring pop of notifications diverts the mind. Turn off notifications. Better still, put your phone in airplane mode. Force yourself to sit down, confront the task and work on it. If it feels tough and you find yourself reaching for your phone, take a quick two-minute walk and come back to give it a go again. Find a quiet space. Tune out the world. Give the task your full attention. Set a timer to, say, thirty minutes. Don't judge your progress. Just get through as much as you can. You will be pleasantly surprised at how much you might get done. If you don't, don't despair. Come back to it again.

Set aside time every day to do your most important task. It must be diarised for it to happen. Jeff Bezos, founder and former CEO of Amazon, does not start meetings till 10:30 a.m. or 11 a.m. He uses his morning time strategically on deep work.

If you have a hard time prioritising your long task list, you may want to use the Eisenhower Matrix. This is a proven task management tool used by thousands of professionals to prioritise your task list. You'll categorise your tasks into four buckets based on urgency and importance: tasks you'll do first, tasks you'll schedule for later, tasks you'll delegate and tasks you'll delete.

Bullet journaling is another method to ensure that all your activity results in achievement and is not frittered away. It involves articulating goals, being conscious about intentions and going about tasks in a focused manner by working backwards from a future view, monthly view and daily view of what needs to be done.

The method you use does not matter. What matters is relentless focus on things that add value and not just things that keep you busy at work.

Developing Range

Something nobody tells you when you start your career is that it is highly beneficial to be a generalist rather than a specialist. Of course, you will always have marketing or finance or your core area as your centre of gravity, but a solid knowledge of other functional areas, other domains and other industries will prove to be very valuable as you ascend in your career. This is why some large organisations have a structured management training programme to rotate freshers across all parts of the company.

When I was younger, people would say I was a jack of all trades and master of none. This didn't bother me too much even though many friends who had chosen their fixed paths were rising to great heights even at a young age. I enjoyed hopping between extracurricular activities such as tennis and swimming, Carnatic music and Bharatanatyam. Neither did my parents push me to choose one to focus on nor did I want to.

Attending a liberal arts college in the US for my undergraduate studies furthered this characteristic of mine to experiment with many different things rather than settle on just one interest or passion. The programme offered at Davidson College allowed me to take studio art, calculus, French, existential philosophy, macroeconomics, Indian art history and these were just a few of the varied courses I took.

Even in business school at SPJIMR, year one was all about exposure to a broad range of topics including finance, marketing, Human Resources, organisational behaviour and operations research (OR) to name a few. It didn't seem valuable at that time (especially OR, which I was not fond of), but I have learned the importance of having some knowledge of the different departments of an organisation irrespective of which one you might end up choosing as your career path.

David Epstein, a *New York Times* best-selling author, calls this 'range'. According to Epstein, this is a critical characteristic of being successful in the 21st century. His research into highly successful professionals across fields shows that generalists and not specialists are best equipped to excel. The big message from his book of the same name, *Range*, is that the more you experiment, the more varied experiences you pick up, the more diverse knowledge you gather. All of these will be hugely beneficial to your career development.

Ever since I became conscious of the importance of range in the workplace, I have been intentionally doing my best to broaden my perspective wherever I can.

I think of range in a very multidimensional way.

Business knowledge

This is about understanding parts of the business which are not your specialisation. As a creative professional, I strive to be up to date on the world of business and finance. When it comes to our clients' businesses, I go the extra mile to understand how different industries work. One year I could be focused on wire rope manufacturing and the next on consumer finance. I might never use some of this knowledge again, but I have learned that creativity works in unique ways. An interesting tidbit about how wire ropes are made in the steel furnace may turn out to be valuable insight for an internal communications campaign for an IT company!

Knowledge in general

Do you read books and magazines only related to your field? Can a home improvement magazine teach you anything about e-commerce platforms? You never know. Developing range is about being widely read across subject areas. Be a voracious reader. Consume everything from astrophysics to gardening. A favourite excursion of mine is to go to the local magazine stand once a month to pick up a broad variety of magazines. I always learn so much, which can be applied later to my projects.

Work experiences

Think about the roles in the organisation where you are working? Is the only way up or are there lateral moves you can make? If you've mastered marketing, why not push yourself outside your comfort zone and give sales a shot? Or perhaps a stint in HR can help you develop empathy, an important skill in senior leadership roles. Choose a variety of roles that can help you develop holistically. If you feel stuck in your current organisation, switch to another company or better still another industry. This too would give you a wider perspective.

While I have stayed in one organisation, I have had many roles across different geographies all of which have contributed to my range. I have done everything from project management to naming to brand strategy and design management in my firm before rising the ranks to my current position.

Life experiences

Think of consciously putting yourself through different experiences in life. It could be classes you sign up for (cooking, dancing, learning a foreign language), trips you go on (venturing beyond the beaten path of the most popular tourist locations in your city or elsewhere) or new cuisines you experiment with. The idea is to fill your mind with a variety of stimuli which become the dots you can connect to develop powerful ideas.

No matter where you are on the spectrum from specialist to generalist, it's never too late to widen the aperture. Exposure to diverse knowledge and varied work and life experiences will become a huge competitive advantage for you.

Feedback

Feedback is one of those weird things that everyone understands is important for progress, but nobody wants to go near it. It's not particularly pleasant to give feedback. You're worried about how the other person will feel, you don't want to offend them or risk coming across as a jerk. It's even more difficult to be at the receiving end of feedback. You want to rush in to defend yourself and clarify what you meant to do or say in a situation. Listening to all the hard things about you, you can't help going into a downward spiral of demotivation from which it may become hard to recover.

If you're a senior person, getting honest feedback becomes even more difficult. Nobody wants to tell you the truth of your actions or expressions. People may vehemently disagree with you, but they may rarely express their views. Even in board meetings, board members (even the independent directors) are reluctant to tell the CEO the truth. In short, nobody likes feedback, but it is essential to growth and progress.

What if there was a magical way to unlock feedback? It turns out there is. All it takes is for us to change the word feedback to advice. Ask, 'Do you have any advice for me?'

Who doesn't like to give advice? Ask for advice and watch the floodgates open. Why is there such a different reaction to the word advice? Claire Lew, CEO of Know Your Team, says that advice is a much more welcoming word than feedback. The latter carries baggage and negative associations. When you ask for advice, the other person is flattered because you are inviting them to share their thoughts and is more likely to open up.

If the above is a cool way to get people to give you feedback, is there a better way to give feedback yourself? Yes.

Have you heard of the praise-to-criticism ratio? The ideal in the workplace is 6:1. For every one criticism you dole out, make sure to give six heaps of praise.

Always start with a lot of praise. Recall all the good things that the person you are giving feedback to is doing. When you start on such a positive note, you are opening them up to receive your feedback.

Then go to make a specific data-backed observation about something that went wrong or a behaviour that is not acceptable at the workplace. Talk them through the impact of this on the colleagues and customers. Suggest a few ways in which this can be handled differently in the future. Be sure to be kind, sincere, specific and clear.

End with a few more points about all that the employee is doing well.

Kim Scott is the queen of 'Radical Candor', a management philosophy based on caring personally while challenging directly. It emphasises the importance of giving direct, honest feedback while showing genuine care for the individual. It is about creating an open communication culture where leaders and team members challenge each other directly and empathetically to drive growth and improvement. By balancing kindness with clear, constructive criticism, Radical Candor fosters trust, boosts performance and cultivates a more engaged and productive workplace.

The feedback styles you want to avoid are manipulative insincerity (when you praise someone to the face but criticise behind the back), ruinous empathy (not giving bad news to avoid short-term pain) and obnoxious aggression (challenging directly without caring personally).

Kim Scott's book by the same name, *Radical Candor*, will help you be a great boss without losing your humanity to help inspire your teams to do the best work of their lives.

2

Body

I DIDN'T START UNDERSTANDING MY body or having a relationship with it until my first year in college in the US. In 1993 when I got hit by 'freshman 15'. I remember being absolutely devastated standing on the scale in my dorm room and discovering I had gained almost seven kilograms in the three months after arriving at Davidson. It was my first time in the United States. I was a vegetarian. The food in the college cafeteria was bland and unappetising. I barely ate at proper mealtimes, which made me easily give in to cookies, pizzas, pop tarts, popcorn and other junk food that students reached for when studying late into the night. I was so jealous of my American college mates, especially the girls. They seemed to binge eat and drink, yet most of them were not packing on the pounds as fast as I was. What was their secret?

I realised that many girls were obsessed with their bodies. I noticed they would ensure they worked out every day. If they were not on one of our college's sports teams like basketball or lacrosse, they would have a disciplined routine of cardio and weight training, which they managed to follow despite a very hectic class schedule. I tried to emulate them. But it just wasn't for me. Even though I was athletic in high school, I was unable to fit sports into my college schedule. I prioritised studying and socialising. I worked part time in my free hours as I had a lot of financial aid from my college. The international students who were my friends were not into exercise either. And I had a long-distance boyfriend who lived on the West Coast (he's my husband now!) whom I chatted with till the wee hours of the morning.

I struggled throughout college to lose my freshman 15. I was not successful. In fact, I gained even more weight in my junior and senior years. I returned to India like a puffed penguin, terribly embarrassed about the weight gain which totally overshadowed the fact that I graduated with honours, majoring in economics with a concentration in applied math. My body had let me down. It was the only visible signal to the world of my four years in America and it wasn't a pretty picture.

After graduating from Davidson College in 1997, I spent a few years in India before heading back to the US to live after I had gotten married in 2000. It was only then that I finally started becoming keenly conscious that I could indeed have a better relationship with my body by following a more holistic approach.

One of our friends in the Bay Area had lost a lot of weight. I was inspired by his tips and suggestions which included having lots of water and adequate sleep, exercising every day and clean eating. I read books, started cooking healthier meals, incorporated exercise into my routine and paid attention to sleep. I was travelling twice a month for work so it wasn't easy to be consistent, but the initial results of my new regime were so positive that I was charged to keep going. My body was finally responding. I was treating it well and being kinder to it and just like that, almost like magic, the kilos started dropping. It was such an incredible high to wake up and not have to fuss too much about what clothes to wear to work because everything made me look fit and fabulous. The challenge was then to maintain my weight and continue to live a healthy life.

I got a few jolts again in 2007 after delivering my first baby and then in 2008 after my second. And it was only after my second baby was a few years old that I finally got into a proper rhythm and started understanding my body and caring for it.

I intuitively knew that I had to master my body to be successful in my profession. I had to look physically fit, but I also needed the physical and mental energy to stay at the top of my game.

I came across a book by Greg Wells called *The Ripple Effect* in which he evangelises the link between health and performance. If you sleep well, you make better eating choices. Eating better fuels your movement and movement impacts thinking. I was sold on this simple philosophy: sleep better, eat better, move better, think better. I practised incorporating healthy habits related to each of these pillars, but then I realised more recently that a big missing component was breathing. I simply had not realised how critical breathing was for my health and ability to perform. James Nestor's seminal book *Breath: The New Science of a Lost Art* shook me up to the critical importance of breath, which should be the first thing anyone should pay attention to.

My biggest lesson over the years has been that if I didn't pay attention to my body and my health, everything else I was doing for my career was futile. This is a realisation that many of us won't have in our twenties. Youth gives us the arrogance to think we have unlimited supplies of energy and good health. But as we live our lives with the busyness and stress that most of us face daily, our health may be slowly eroding away without it being visible. Please pay attention to your body – protect it and nurture it before it is too late.

Breathing Techniques

If I have one genuine regret on how I was brought up, it is that my parents did not teach me how to breathe properly. Wait, what? Does such a thing even exist? That there is a proper way to breathe? Turns out there is, as espoused by James Nestor in his book *Breath*.

The biggest insight I took away from Nestor's book is that most human beings have lost the art of breathing. Many of us breathe through our mouths instead of through our noses. We don't take deep breaths as often as we need to, and we are not aware of the importance of keeping our olfactory pathways clear. The nose filters the air, warms it, humidifies it and produces nitric oxide which is good for our health. It helps to increase blood flow and reduce blood pressure. If you or your loved ones have ever experienced snoring, sleep apnoea, dental issues, lung issues and a host of other ailments, you may want to examine and fix your breathing before you do anything else.

James warns us that it doesn't matter how healthy we are in other aspects. If we're not breathing properly then nothing else matters. He draws on thousands of years of medical research as well as recent scientific studies in pulmonology, psychology, biochemistry and human physiology to make a strong argument for the power of breath.

Our caveman ancestors didn't snore. Modern humans are the only species with chronically crooked teeth. We are the worst breathers in the animal kingdom. These are some of the more memorable facts I learned from the book.

The book introduced me to tried and tested breathing techniques that have been practised in Hinduism, Buddhism, Christianity and other religions for aeons. It is only now that humans have a deeper understanding of how our breathing impacts blood pressure, our nervous system and our ability to perform athletically.

I certainly never breathed the same again after reading James' book. Did I rush to learn ancient practices like sudarshan kriya, tummo and others? No. But I did double down on pranayama and concentrated on this more in my twice-a-week yoga sessions. I also used the Mindfulness app on my Apple Watch to keep track of my HRV (heart rate variability) through the day. The Mindfulness app offers modes like 'Reflect' and 'Breathe', which I have found extremely helpful in ensuring I take regular breaks to slow down and to practise deep breathing and breath holding.

The 'Reflect' mode offers sessions lasting from one to five minutes. Pick a duration and then sit back comfortably. Closing your eyes is optional. What's important is to pay attention to the sensations in your body. The app prompts you to begin the session with one or two slow breaths to ease your mind and reflect on the prompt. Examples of prompts include: think of a challenge and how it will make you grow; remember a moment when someone was kind to you and how that made you feel. At the end of the session, you are encouraged to carry the calm and stillness into your day. The 'Breathe' mode is simply a timer and vibration that allows you to modulate your deep breathing for a selected duration (same as above).

There are many benefits of breathing properly that I noticed in my life.

Reduced anxiety

I have every reason to be stressed all day. I have a hectic schedule to manage at work. And two teenagers at home. Something or the other keeps popping up which can escalate my blood pressure if I am not conscious. Regular two-minute breath intervals throughout the day helps me operate at an equanimous state at most times.

Better sleep

I try to practise deep breathing for five to ten minutes before going to sleep at night. This has completely changed the quality of my sleep as I now usually wake up well-rested and without an alarm at the same time every morning. Even at night, if I am disturbed by nature's call or for some other reason, a few minutes of deep breathing helps me go back to sleep.

More energy while exercising

Breathing has made all the difference to my endurance during exercising, whether that is walking, running, yoga, tennis or weight training. I usually look up the right technique of breathing with various exercises to make sure I am doing it correctly. With conscious breathing techniques, I feel I am not only doing my exercise better but I'm also able to do it longer.

Reduced yawning

I used to be a chronic yawner even after a night of good sleep. How could that be possible? I learned that one of the common causes of yawning is stress and anxiety. Here too regular deep breathing has helped me reduce yawning greatly.

Being sharper through the day

I have noticed that on days when I am very consciously deep breathing at regular intervals, my brain feels like it is charged up and ready to fire on all cylinders. Oxygen to the brain improves blood circulation, enhancing cognitive performance, focus and mental clarity.

Posture

I had terrible posture while growing up. Frankly, it's another area where my parents could have taught me better! I have found that breathing has helped me become more conscious of not slouching. Proper breathing helps engage the diaphragm and deep core muscles, which supports spinal alignment and overall body mechanics.

Digestion

Who knew that breathing can also improve digestion? This happens through the activation of the vagus nerve when you breathe properly. The vagus nerve can trigger the relaxation response of your nervous system which enables proper digestion. Breathing correctly during eating has also prevented many a binge meal for me. Mindfulness in eating is a huge benefit to breathing properly.

There are many breathing techniques that you can learn depending on how deep you want to go. Here are some that I have tried:
Alternate nostril breathing (Nadi shodhana): This yogic breathing technique is believed to balance the energy in the body, enhance mental clarity and promote relaxation. I practise this twice a week during my yoga sessions.
Kapalabhati (Skull-shining breath): This is another yogic breathing technique known to cleanse and energise the body, improve mental focus and invigorate the respiratory system. I pair this with nadi shodhana during my yoga classes.
Box breathing: It is commonly used to calm the mind, reduce anxiety and promote focus. I use box breathing as the key technique for my two-minute breathing breaks through the day.
4-7-8 breathing: Developed by Dr Andrew Weil, this technique is often used to induce relaxation, reduce stress and aid in falling asleep. I use this technique for five-or ten-minute sessions.

You reap many benefits from just breathing properly! Breathing has been a game changer for me. I only wish I had known about it from the day I was born.

Managing Your Energy

Earlier in the book I talked about the importance of time management. While this is a necessary foundational skill to succeed in the workplace, it will not help you if you don't have the energy for your carefully planned day. What is even more important than managing your time is managing your energy.

While good time management has helped me squeeze a lot into my days, I have found that on the days when I manage my energy properly, I don't feel exhausted at all. I may have woken up at 4 a.m. for a 6 a.m. flight to Delhi, attended business meetings all day, then reached home well past 10 p.m. Yet I was energised throughout the day and even woke up on time the next morning, squeezed in my workout and was at my desk by 9 a.m. My colleagues used to wonder where I got this energy from. It seemed to them I was never tired. I have the occasional day or two in a year when I may call in sick, but most of my long-time colleagues won't be able to recall a time when I was sick for more than a day or two. They may recall the time I fractured my knee on a ski trip to Gulmarg and was on crutches for several months. Or they may recall the day after my first Covid-19 vaccine when I was deathly sick in bed! But nothing beyond that.

I passionately believe that the foundation of energy management is good health. The words of my paediatrician telling me, in the early years of my two daughters, that 'health is wealth' ring in my ears often. I didn't pay attention then, but now, and especially after the experience of the pandemic, I know that health is everything. If you don't have good health, it will be hard to go far in your career. Your health is the silent and invisible enabler that powers you.

Like every aspect I have talked about in the book, it comes down to routine and habits. I have incorporated a few things into my lifestyle that have helped me manage my energy throughout the day.

There are two categories – energy givers and energy drainers. I simply try to maximise my time with energy givers and minimise my time with energy drainers.

What gives me energy?

Rising with the sun. I'm a fan of syncing my body with its circadian rhythm. I am usually up by 6 a.m. Earlier in my career my morning would begin by 4 a.m. and 5 a.m. to get quiet work done.

My morning workout. I exercise for at least an hour every morning – weight training thrice a week, yoga twice a week, tennis once a week. Sunday is usually a rest day. If I come back early in the evening, I squeeze in an evening walk for at least half an hour, though I try to push for one. Robin Sharma is a big advocate of getting into two workouts if possible.

Eating healthy foods and staying hydrated. I consume plenty of vegetables at every meal. Even at breakfast I have a salad with eggs or raw veggies with sprouts. I drink a lot of water throughout the day and have very little caffeine.

Lots of hugs and cuddles with my daughters. Moments with them always energise me.

A motivating conversation with a close person. A conversation with my husband or a close friend or a phone call to my mom or dad is particularly invigorating.

Listening to music. Listening to my favourite playlist on Spotify while I get ready for work livens up my day.

Dressing well. When I look good, I feel good. I make it a point to take care of how I dress. When I am sharply dressed, I am even more energised to conquer my day.

Priming for my day on my ride to the office. I like thinking about the tasks at hand, honing in on the one thing to which I can add the most value.

Smiling and being friendly with everyone I meet. Shaking hands, a pat on the back, a quick chat – each friendly exchange with a colleague puts a spring in my step.

Watching my language. Words have transformative power. Always look forward, without blaming anyone. 'No worries,' 'We can do this,' 'How might we tackle this issue?', 'Who can help us?' – the right choice of words keeps my mood upbeat and positive when tackling challenging situations at work.

Group brainstorms. The energy of diverse minds collaborating to solve problems gives me energy too!

Expressing gratitude. I find myself feeling happy when I compliment others and thank them for a good job done. I know it will make them feel good and that in turn uplifts me as well.

What drains my energy?

Too much sugar. When I am tempted by cakes, jalebis and all the other goodies at work, I can feel the highs and lows through the day, and they don't feel great at all.

Negative people. Some people just can't stop complaining. They always imagine the worst-case scenario. They may be spreading negativity. This is one of the things that I am not fond of. I try hard to navigate away from negative people.

Sitting too much. It sounds counterintuitive, but it's on days when I am moving the most between meetings is when I feel the most energised. Sitting all day in front of the laptop is one of the biggest energy drainers.

Doom-scrolling on my mobile. Despite my busy schedule, I too turn to LinkedIn or Instagram, scrolling way more often than I should. It's an activity I should avoid more because it leaves me feeling dull and drained.

Dehydration. I try my best to stay hydrated through the day, going through 3–4 litres of water on most days. When I travel or when I am stressed, I turn more to tea and food. Bad idea. Less water is linked to lower energy levels for me.

Lack of sleep. My body needs at least seven hours of rest. I fooled myself into thinking I only needed six earlier in my career, but these days I push to seven even eight hours of sleep at night. It makes a massive difference in my energy levels the next day. When I am well-rested, I have unlimited energy for the day, unless I indulge in any of the energy drainers!

No matter where you are in your journey of managing your energy, it would be a good idea to list the energy givers and the energy drainers in your life. And then it's a matter of awareness first and then action. You must keep balancing out the equation to ensure that you are net energy positive at all times.

Restful Sleep

Many years ago, when I was working in our London office, we were engaged by a large pharmaceutical company on the naming and branding of a sleeping pill. A lot of the ideas revolved around how this pill helped you sleep better, sleep longer, sleep more comfortably, sleep more peacefully and so forth. However these themes were not differentiated at all against all the other brands in the market. We needed to think about sleep differently. Then one day, our creative director had a breakthrough. He said we were focused on the wrong thing. You don't take a sleeping pill just to sleep better. The whole point of it was to wake up brighter! The penny dropped and we went on to successfully win the client over with our solutions.

I remember this story vividly because it changed my perspective on sleep. The reason to be disciplined about sleep is to have energy for your day's ambitions. Without your battery being fully charged and ready to go after a full night's deep sleep, you would go nowhere.

Around this time, I was introduced to two life-changing books by Arianna Huffington, *Thrive: The Third Metric to Redefining Success and Creating a Life of Well-Being, Wisdom, and Wonder* and *The Sleep Revolution: Transforming Your Life, One Night at a Time*. These books were published in a span of two years. I read them back-to-back. Nothing I had read thus far had the transformational impact on me as did the work of Arianna Huffington.

Thrive was a real eye-opener to the fact that I was going down the path of being a workaholic who did not prioritise my health or well-being. I was a working mom of two toddlers, juggling parenting and professional duties. I used to travel for work at least once a week. It would be a day trip to Delhi, Bangalore, Kolkata, Hyderabad, Pune or Chennai.

Weekends were fully devoted to the girls. But there was never much downtime and hardly any time for exercise. High stress due to the constant balancing act meant that I made poor food choices. All of this added up and I often felt like I was running on empty just like Arianna had been when she fell from exhaustion at her desk, which resulted in a broken cheekbone and a nasty gash on her eye. Her horrific experience and overarching message connected with me deeply. What was I chasing? What was my definition of success? Would I pursue it at any cost to my well-being?

Arianna helped me understand that there's much more to life than professional achievement. Money and power are two legs of a three-legged stool that will topple over in the long run if you don't have a third leg. That third leg, according to Arianna, is the ability to 'thrive'. Thriving is a big idea that encompasses one's ability to be deeply connected to oneself. The four pillars of being able to thrive are: well-being, wisdom, wonder and giving.

This newfound awareness made me realise what terrible habits I had. I used to sleep within an hour of eating. I was on my phone or my laptop until the second I fell asleep. Often, I would drink a glass of red wine before going to bed. And of course, I would carry all my tensions about the day and worries about the next to bed with me. Wrong. Wrong. Wrong. None of these meant I was getting good quality sleep. Quality over quantity is what I learned. That REM sleep is necessary not only for your body to rest but also for your brain to detoxify. The brain needs as much cleaning as our physical body and sleep is one way in which the brain cleans up and gets fresh for the next day.

Slowly, I started changing my habits. I didn't fix everything all at once but my deep dive into the importance of sleep did introduce me to a few practices that have helped me immensely.

Here are some of the practices:

Eating three hours before bed

There are numerous benefits to eating before sunset but the biggest one for me is that my food would be digested by the time I went to sleep which is usually around 10. It wasn't that difficult because when you have young kids, your life does revolve around them. The tough part was (and continues to be) not eating after dinner and before bed. Not snacking in those three to four hours can be challenging. Sometimes I crave a dessert. Other times a drink. It can also be just mindless snacking. I have learned to stay disciplined, and it has helped me maintain a proper night's sleep.

Switching off digital devices an hour before bed

Arianna's team developed a bed for your mobile phone. She recommends keeping your phone in a phone bed in a room other than the bedroom where you sleep. She suggests a ritual of putting your phone to bed at least an hour before you go to sleep. And no popping into the bedroom at night on the way back from the washroom or for any other reason. This practice will dramatically improve the quality of your sleep.

Digital devices are the biggest enemies of sound sleep. The light from the devices interferes with the natural melatonin-forming process in your body. And when you check your phone in the middle of the night, your brain is woken up and your worries will take over. While I am unable to keep my phone in another room (I'm always worried about missing an emergency call from my daughters or my parents), I don't look at it at all at night. And I do try to switch off at least forty-five minutes before bed. Sometimes it's hard because there is always a string of to-dos to complete but I know I'm compromising on my sleep every time I do this.

Writing in my journal
This is an excellent method for unloading all my thoughts onto the page. Once I have put down my thoughts, I feel much lighter. Some days I write whatever comes to mind. On other days I practise gratitude journaling. The act of writing itself slows me down.

A warm shower/bath
This is my most reliable sleep inducer. If I use natural essential oils like lavender vanilla, I can visualise deep sleep even when I am in my bath. This is followed by moisturising my body with a cream that has sleep-inducing essential oils and I'm all set. I usually have soft calming music in the background to de-stress me as well.

Stretches and deep breathing
The second last thing I do before switching off completely is to practise a few stretches. I have found many routines on the Internet which have been very helpful. Even just ten minutes of legs up against the wall does the job. I make it a point to practise two to five minutes of deep breathing. This one is very important to ensure the quality of my sleep at night.

There's so much to be learned about everything one can do to get deep sleep which prepares you for the day ahead. Don't be intimidated by all the wisdom and well-meaning advice on this topic. Absorb all the material and then pick two to three things that you feel are most relevant and can be applied in your life.

Nutrition

When I saw the title of one of nutritionist Rujuta Diwekar's books, *Women and the Weight Loss Tamasha*, I had a hearty laugh. I haven't read the book, but I can very much relate to the title.

My relationship with my body was based on just one metric: my weight. When it was down, I felt elated. When it started climbing up, my sense of self-worth plummeted. I knew no other way to gauge if I was healthy or not. This one number seemed to be the be-all and end-all of health as I was seeing it. Oh, how wrong I was! It was not until recently that I stopped weighing myself, unless I had to for my annual medical check-up. Or the odd occasion when you have no choice but to stand on the scales, like when we were boarding a small propeller plane from Mahé airport in the Seychelles to go to one of the island resorts – the airline operator had to ensure that the passenger load balance was correct to allow the plane to lift-off. It was a stark reminder of the importance of staying lightweight in life.

What I have learned over the years is that nutrition is a holistic concept. It is medicine for your body. The right, healthy food nourishes the body and gives it the energy it needs to function on a biological level. But food also impacts the brain. What we eat has a profound influence on how we think and how we feel. The adage 'you are what you eat' is true after all!

My learnings about nutrition over the years have been informed by books, TV shows, coaching with nutritionists and now, social media. I have amassed a lot of knowledge in this area but it's always about the daily practical application that makes a positive difference given my hectic lifestyle.

If you only had time for a cup of tea with me, what might I share with you that could be useful and motivating for your health journey? All that has worked for me and what have I adopted in my lifestyle.

What follows are ten key learnings about nutrition that I hope you find easy, sensible and impactful.

Eat less

An overarching principle I follow is to avoid stuffing myself. Of all the advice I have heard and assimilated, this is probably the most transformational. It is the easiest to understand and yet the most difficult to practise. They say you have two ears and a mouth – listen more and talk less. Similarly, I say you have two eyes and one mouth. Feast all you want with your eyes but be mindful of what is going in through your mouth.

There are some tricks to follow here. Fill up your plate only once and don't take seconds. You should apply this rule at every meal at home and especially when you eat out, particularly at buffets. If you are still hungry, give it twenty minutes before you dig in again. The signal from your stomach to your brain takes that much time. If your hunger persists, then reach for the seconds. Most times, it will pass.

Have a full glass of water half an hour before your meal. Learn to distinguish between hunger and thirst. When you reach for that candy bar are you hungry or just thirsty?

Learn to understand your body better. Are you eating because your body needs it? Or are you eating because of anxiety or even boredom? The thing to avoid at all costs is binge eating. Just don't do it. Wedding season or Diwali are just excuses. The damage that binge eating inflicts on your digestive system is severe and takes months if not years to recover.

Chew your food well

When I lived in France for six months during undergrad, I noticed how the French ate small meals but took inordinate amounts of time for each meal. I observed that they chewed every morsel, and their style of eating was unlike anything I had seen in India until then. This principle is about using all your teeth (especially the molars) to grind your food well and prepare it for smooth digestion. This pace also allows the necessary time for the satiety signals to reach the brain from the stomach, which will prevent overeating.

Two minutes of deep breathing before a meal

Breathing anchors me in the present moment. This helps to avoid eating for the wrong reasons and to concentrate on the meal. It allows me to scan the table or the menu to make the right choices. Most importantly, it prevents emotional eating. When I was in my mid-forties I had signed up for a three-month consultation with Tara Mahadevan, a Mumbai-based nutritional psychologist. From her, I learned about the intimate connection between your mind and what you eat. You must be in a calm and relaxed state before eating. Breathing helps you arrive at that state.

A balanced plate

I have been on many diets. I used to hate carbs. I thought they were evil. At one point, I avoided fats altogether. All those strategies were wrong. What's important is a balance of the three macronutrients our bodies need – carbohydrates, proteins, and fat. One simple method I learned from Madhuri Ruia, a nutritionist, is to fill half your plate with vegetables, a quarter with protein and a quarter with carbs. Loading up on vegetables not only provides good roughage for digestion but also fills you up nicely. The more colourful your plate, the better. Eat the rainbow! Broccoli, spinach, purple cabbage, carrots, tomatoes and butternut squash are just some of the varied colours you can incorporate.

The order matters

Jessie Inchauspé, who goes by @glucosegoddess on Instagram, is an author and social media phenomenon who has combed through gigabytes of research from all over the world to study the impact of blood sugar on our metabolism. Her findings teach us that the order in which you eat your macronutrients matters. Most of us are overstressing our mitochondria because of sugar overload. And by sugar, I mean glucose sugar, which is contained in carbohydrates as well. What she advocates is for us to eat vegetables first because they line up the stomach and help in better absorption of the food that comes after. Protein should be eaten next followed by carbohydrates.

Even if you ate the same amounts of all three, the order in which you eat them makes a huge difference in how you process the food.

The objective is to avoid sudden rises in your glucose levels called spikes. A glucose spike is a rapid increase in blood sugar levels that typically occurs after consuming foods high in sugar or simple carbohydrates. Short-term effects include fatigue, irritability and even hunger, causing you to overeat. Long-term effects include weight gain, insulin resistance and the risk of heart disease.

Inchauspé recommends that fats and carbs must be paired with proteins. A cupcake causes a sharp spike but pair the cupcake with some Greek yogurt and the spike is more evenly spaced out. I usually have a small bag of nuts or seeds lying around. I sprinkle seeds like sesame and pumpkin over my salads and fruit plates. I also try to have a few almonds or walnuts with dessert.

Follow the sun

You'll see the importance of the circadian rhythm pop up a few times in this book. It's most important to follow when it comes to your food. Heavy meals at night, eaten after sunset, is the worst thing you can do to your body. What is the logic behind this? If you eat late and sleep shortly after that, your body has very little time to digest the food and it will just rot in your stomach overnight. Your sleep will be impacted, and you won't wake up with the energy you need to conquer your day. Most likely, you will reach for caffeine hit after caffeine hit to keep you going, which leads to crashes of energy that can be detrimental to your day.

The healthiest routine to follow is to space your three meals between sunrise and sunset. They should be balanced meals. A light meal at night is encouraged to aid digestion. I follow this regularly and can see the negative impact the next day if I have had a night out and eaten late. If you must binge a bit, do it at lunch. Your body will have plenty of time to digest it, assuming you aren't sedentary all afternoon after a heavy lunch.

Eat fresh and wholesome foods

I used to travel almost twice a week for many years until recently. I loved the cuppa noodles, upma and veg biryani on Indigo flights until I learned how terrible they are for your health. Ayurveda has a concept of 'dead food' which says that three hours after food is prepared, it is no longer good for your body. I don't take this literally, but it has hugely turned me off packaged foods, pre-prepared foods on flights, frozen foods and even leftovers, all of which were staples in my diet. I understand the value of freshly prepared home-cooked food because I can feel the positive energy these foods give me versus the slight heaviness that comes with eating foods that have gone stale. I have minimised the use of frozen, canned and packaged food at home. I also try to avoid too many sauces and pickles because of the same reason.

Intermittent fasting

I came late to this party but am a full convert now. We stuff ourselves too much. Along with the first principle of eating less, it is also a good idea to give your body regular breaks from digestion. In our crazy 24/7, always-on world, we are also unconsciously subjecting our bodies to non-stop digestion because of the food and snacks we are constantly feeding it.

I have tried 12-hour and 16-hour fasts. What works best for me is 7 p.m. to 7 a.m. the next morning, sometimes stretching to 10 or 11 a.m. I try to follow this a few times a week and am working towards incorporating this into my everyday routine. Some people fast regularly once a week or once a month for religious reasons – this also tells us how our ancestors sensed the need for regular breaks for our body from digestion and therefore built these rituals into our culture. Intermittent fasting has a boatload of benefits including prevention of ageing, which is a big one for me. Who doesn't want to do everything to remain young forever?

Hydration matters

Very closely linked with nutrition is your water intake. Most of us would know by now that regular water intake throughout the day is important. Some may follow the eight glasses a day rule. Others aim for three to four litres, especially if you live in tropical climates. I have found a direct correlation between my regular water intake and food choices. On the days when I am consciously consuming the required water intake, I eat healthier.

When I travel or am stressed at work, I reach for cups of tea and junk food more often. The amount of water I drink reduces. I feel terrible at the end of the day. Water is your best companion at work and in life. What I do is ensure that I always have a bottle of water next to me and I'm taking some sips throughout the day. I have an app on my phone in which I record my intake to ensure I reach my 4 litres-a-day goal since I exercise every day as well. During Covid-19, I discovered the benefits of warm water. It is very satiating and helps manage hunger pangs if you sip warm water through the day. The movement of water through your body keeps the blood circulating and helps in carrying the nutrients to the right places.

Enjoy every meal

While there are hundreds of dos and don'ts around nutrition, it is important to not be inundated with all the advice. Avoid going on crash diets or unrealistic meal plans that call for cabbage soup all day. These are neither practical nor sustainable. I have become an ardent disciple of Luke Coutinho, who evangelises the holistic lifestyle method where nutrition is one pillar of four. The other three are movement, sleep and stress management.

When it comes to nutrition, my philosophy is gratitude and enjoyment of every meal. Being present, scanning with my eyes before eating and then enjoying every morsel of the portions I have served myself is what works for me. I do enjoy different kinds of food and at one point in time I would have considered myself a 'foodie' but I have learned that it gives too much importance to just one pillar of my holistic lifestyle.

I also don't want to live dreaming about every upcoming meal and making bucket lists of restaurants to visit. I'm not saying it's wrong. I've just stopped doing that. Of course, we are all incredibly privileged to have the abundance we do. I will never forget the millions of people who don't have a square meal a day. That sensitivity and gratitude for what I have keeps me on track to fully enjoy my every meal.

Physical Fitness

If you have nightmares about physical exercise class in school, you are not alone. While I was a sporty child, I hated being pulled out of class on a hot day, getting all sweaty running around the quad and then staying in my sweaty PE clothes for the rest of the day. That could have put me off exercise forever but for college when I saw my peers taking a key interest in regular exercise. It made me understand that PE is an important component of a healthy adult lifestyle.

When I started working, I almost stopped exercising. I was so enamoured by the world of work. I wanted to impress my bosses. I put in long hours and there was no time left for exercise. Combine this with the knowledge worker's curse of sitting behind a desk all day and you have a time bomb ticking. I see this happening all the time with my younger colleagues. People get so absorbed into work and the quest for achievement that they don't even think about their health until something tragic happens. We just don't realise at the peak of our youth that lack of exercise or, more simply, movement is linked with all sorts of age-related diseases one could get including diabetes, cardiovascular issues, cancer, arthritis, dementia, Parkinson's to name a few.

A few incidents changed my perspective on the value of exercising every day. And now I am a lifer. I barely go through a day without some form or other of medium intensity exercise, whether it is walking, running, yoga, weight training, tennis or swimming.

So how did I go from a young employee who spent zero minutes on exercise to the senior leader who devotes at least sixty minutes a day, often more, to physical activity?

My first shock came when I started working at Landor in San Francisco. I was newly married. I was starry-eyed about work and as a result, neglected the importance of a healthy lifestyle. Frankly, I was so obsessed with my career that I was not even aware that I was compromising my health every day with my sedentary lifestyle.

A year into working, I had gained about 10 kg. None of my clothes fit. I started looking downright dowdy in a very stylish agency. I felt crappy every morning when I looked in the mirror. Something had to change. I turned to *SHAPE* magazine for motivation. I remembered some of my college friends being ardent fans. I started reading the magazine regularly. I enjoyed every issue from cover to cover but it didn't make me get off my chair.

Three or four months into reading the magazine regularly, I came across an article that suggested I didn't need to have an elaborate workout routine or join a fancy gym. I just needed to choose an activity like running and spend at least twenty minutes a day doing it. That's it. The article even suggested I keep my running clothes, shoes and socks by the side of my bed so I could get into them the minute I woke up. I could choose to go out, run for a minute or two and then come back. The only rule was to get ready and go out for a run. And I had to do it every day without fail for thirty days.

It sounded like a reasonable challenge and one I could get through without too much of a fuss, so I gave it a go. On the first day, I exceeded my twenty minutes. I was elated. This is easy-breezy I thought to myself. Then the reality of day two hit me. I didn't even feel like getting out of bed. I was sore. I wanted to sleep in. But I could not give up so early, so I forced myself to get up, get dressed and get outdoors. It was a bit nippy in Redwood City where we used to live. That made me start running so I could stay warm. I ran for about ten minutes and then turned back, came home and went back to sleep for a bit.

The next day was a little easier, and you know what, it got easier and easier as the days passed. I was even mildly optimistic that I might get to my thirty-day target without too much strain. And I did. What were the outcomes? I felt infinitely better every day. I had a lot of energy during the day. I was pairing this with healthier diet as well. The twin forces of more movement and less food helped me lose weight, tone my body and stay positive.

I kept up a healthy lifestyle until I had my daughters. My recovery after my second delivery was particularly tough. I went in to see my anaesthesiologist after four weeks thinking there some was mistake made when administering my epidural during childbirth because my lower back was in excruciating pain. I could barely stand. What have these pregnancies and deliveries done to me, I thought to myself, hugely regretting my decision to have two kids in quick succession who were eighteen months apart. The anaesthesiologist laughed off my suggestion that the epidural might have been wrongly administered. He told me to stop moping around and to start moving throughout the day. 'Get off your butt' was exactly what he said, albeit in a polite manner. Specifically, he recommended yoga.

A colleague knew of a company that sent yoga teachers home and that's how I got started. Two months of yoga three days a week improved my posture, solved my lower back pain and got me addicted to yoga for the rest of my life. While I am extremely restless, yoga calms me, stills my mind and stretches my body in ways that reduce my anxiety and radiate positivity.

A decade later, another incident made me realise the importance of weight training. One winter holiday, I had a mild fracture while skiing in Phase 2 of the Gulmarg ski slopes. I was a decent skier but a smug attitude on slopes that required a lot of skill contributed to my accident. Concentration and focus are critical when you are skiing and I lost both for a split second, which is when I crashed and fractured my left knee. I was on crutches for almost two months, unable to exercise.

A kind physiotherapist who came home a few times a week to get me back on track pointed out that my muscles were weak overall and that the two months on crutches were going to further weaken them. He explained to me that weight training is critical to keep muscles fit which prevents injuries as one gets older. You can reduce cardio but must increase time spent on weight training. You may be put off by the sound of weight training. You don't have to join a gym or use fancy machines. You can buy basic equipment for home including resistance bands, dumbbells and kettlebells and find a routine on YouTube that fits your level of fitness.

My ski accident was also eye-opening in another way. It did not feel good to be handicapped in this manner. I felt like my freedom had been taken away. This incident helped me emotionally connect to what happens when exercise as a privilege is taken away. Being immobile and dependent on others was a loss of freedom and autonomy. Walking around with a crutch made me deeply empathise with those with disabilities and how our society treats them. Being couped up indoors and lack of exercise took a toll on my mental health as it built up my anxiety and made me more irritable. All this helped me understand that I must ensure that I use my privilege as long as I have it because you never know when it might go away. This was a much-needed philosophical enlightenment on the value of exercise.

My latest understanding of exercise is that it's not enough to do it just once a day for an hour or so. If you end up sitting the rest of the day, the exercise is as good as not having done so. Being stuck at home during Covid-19 brought this understanding into sharp focus. I would wake up at the crack of dawn and finish an hour of working out even before the rest of the house woke up. But once work started by 8 a.m., I was glued to my desk till 8 or 9 p.m. at times. Back-to-back Zoom calls meant that you barely walked around except to go to the washroom when you had a few minutes between virtual meetings.

There was hardly any time to even stand and stretch. I paid a heavy price for this. Even after six months of exercise every day I didn't feel great because all that sitting during the day was negating the positive impact of an hour of exercise in the morning. Then, one day, I attended a company-organised online desk yoga class. This is when I realised the importance of getting up and moving every half hour or one hour. It was also important to stretch every part of the body. Moving for at least five to ten minutes every hour was needed. I was not doing any of this. I used to feel exhausted by the evening time. I would eat early but then feel sleepy right after my last call. It felt so unfair that I was working out every day but not getting the desired results and now I knew why. Movement all day is more important than at a fixed hour in the morning or evening.

People ask me how I have so much energy for all the things I do. My answer is simple: I exercise every day. Exercising regularly has given me the stamina to have long days which exert my body and my mind. I no longer get colds and fevers as much as I used to as a child and as a teenager. Exercise has built up my immunity tremendously. In some ways I feel that regular exercise is a surprising determinant of career success. It not only safeguards your health but also gives you the much-needed energy to match your fiery ambition.

Madhuri Ruia, author and nutritionist, on taking care of your body

Hello, all you beautiful women out there!

Your health is a beautiful gift that you bestow upon yourself every day. It is only when you are healthy every day that you can do your best in all areas of your life, not just at work but also in your interactions with family and friends. This is because being free of health worries gives you more time and efficiency. First, it gives you sustained, untiring energy, allowing you to always show up at work, think on your feet in tough situations, and at the same time, cope with responsibilities at home. Second, it gives you more hours in a day because when you are healthy, you approach every task thoughtfully, do more work in less time, and make quick, sharp decisions easily.

Before delving into lifelong habits, let us explore the three essential elements your body needs for optimal health:

1. Consistent Nutrient Supply: Ensure a regular intake of nutritious food and hydration every three to four hours. This provides your brain with a steady flow of essential nutrients,

water and glucose for optimal performance. Prolonged periods without wholesome meals, over-drinking coffee and skipping meals can lead to unbearable hunger pangs and unhealthy food cravings. It's when you give in to such cravings that you end up with sharp spikes and valleys in nutrient and glucose supply, preventing the brain from functioning optimally for you.

2. Natural Nutrients for Energy: Opt for natural nutrients to fuel your body's energy and stamina. Processed and synthetic foods lack the natural components that the body can efficiently utilise, often causing the body to accumulate more fat. To maintain a healthy weight you need to prioritise whole, unprocessed foods over packaged alternatives.
3. Incorporate Movement into Your Day: Cultivate the habit of moving throughout the day to burn the calories you consume. Even healthy, natural food choices can contribute to fat accumulation if unused. Regular physical activity helps maintain a healthy balance between calories consumed and calories expended.

Now, let's discuss the habits that ensure your body works in harmony with your goals:

1. Embrace the 80/20 Rule: Make 80 per cent of your meals home-cooked and wholesome, consisting of natural ingredients like vegetables and fruit, grains, spices, yoghurt and nuts and seeds. This 80 per cent instils dietary discipline effortlessly, leaving room for the occasional indulgence with the remaining 20 per cent from outside sources.
2. Exercise as Medicine: Recognise exercise as a powerful form of medicine. The nutrients from your food, combined with the oxygen supplied through movement, set the gold standard for your health. Exercise promotes cellular health, aids weight management, helps shape your body, improves your mirror image, and boosts self-confidence, all at once.
3. Prioritise Rest and Recovery: Establish a consistent sleep schedule, aiming for bedtime between 10 and 11 p.m. and waking up between 6:00 and 7:00 a.m. This natural rhythm allows your body to reset efficiently, providing mental clarity, supporting digestion and fostering emotional well-being.

4. Stay Hydrated: Ensure proper hydration alongside regular meals. Water is essential for digestion, nutrient absorption, and overall bodily and brain functions.
5. Mindful Eating: Practise mindful eating to savour your food and for a rich sensory experience, recognise hunger and fullness cues and make healthier choices based on how you feel internally in the moment.
6. Social Connection: Nurture strong social ties for emotional support and stress reduction. Stress reduction helps prevent comfort eating to maintain a healthy weight.
7. Mindset: Cultivate a positive outlook, focusing on solutions and maximising potential with the energy you get from staying healthy. Remember, your health journey is unique to you. Listen to your body and adapt as needed.

3

Soul

It's easy to understand and rationalise the importance of developing your mind and keeping your body fit for your career. The lesser talked about pillar of holistic development, which in my mind is the most important, is the nurturing of the soul. If you can tap into your emotions and use them to your advantage, you can truly set yourself apart.

Gratitude sets the stage for positive energy, while empathy and emotional intelligence foster deeper connections in personal and professional relationships. Cultivating joy and embracing authenticity create a psychologically rich life, intertwining threads of genuine expression and vulnerability.

In this section I introduce the idea of being a 'lovecat', emphasising the power of love and compassion in leadership and collaboration. Together, these elements weave a narrative of self-awareness, genuine connections and a purposeful existence.

This section is a journey into the soul, guiding you toward a harmonious balance that not only enhances personal well-being but also serves as a catalyst for career success.

Gratitude

My earliest memory of gratitude is from the seventh grade when I was a new girl at Queen Mary's School in Mumbai and we used to recite 'The Lord's Prayer' during the school assembly. Soon, this Christian prayer became my go-to prayer when I had exams or was in a tough spot and wanted God's help. This was despite being the daughter of a devout Hindu father, albeit a liberal one who did not force his rituals on me. The school forced me to learn the prayer and say it every day. My father did not. Perhaps that had consequences he may not be very happy about.

I stuck with this prayer right up to college when a philosophy class on Existentialism made me question religion as a concept. While I did mechanically recite the prayer, I never got into the habit of being grateful for the abundance and good things in my life. It was a crutch (as some of the philosophers said it was) and one I seemed to lean on only in hours of need.

Gratitude as a concept came into my life during Covid-19. It was tough being cooped up at home with my husband and teenage daughters. He was like a caged bird who just could not reconcile with the confinement and was taking out his frustration on us. The timing couldn't have been worse for my teenage daughters – just when they needed less of us and less parenting overall, they got more of us and more parenting because we were around and could monitor them 24/7, something we could not have done earlier in our busy working lives. This created a pressure cooker-like situation at home with everyone snappy and on edge all the time. I had the additional pressure of running my office from home. When our company offered free one-hour online sessions with a therapist based in Hong Kong to address mental health issues for our staff, I grabbed the opportunity.

My life coach was an energetic, calming and very inspiring lady by the name of Louise Corbett. Originally from Australia, she had settled down in Hong Kong. She used to work in the corporate world, but coaching was her life's calling so she had pivoted her career during Covid-19. Louise listened to all my woes patiently. Her empathetic tone, paraphrasing of what I was saying to make sure I was heard and well understood, follow-up questions and keen interest made me open up to her fully. Even though we were chatting for the first time, I trusted her implicitly.

I learned two things from Louise, which have stayed with me and have had a profound impact on the way I think.

The first is the interconnectedness between work and home. Personal and professional lives are not as compartmentalised as we may think or want them to be. Unhappiness at home carries through into the workplace and vice versa. You can't be a different person at work and at home. The impact of this realisation is that to thrive at work you have to have fulfilling relationships at home. Any unrest or imbalance is bound to negatively affect your performance and your chances of progress in your career. While this made sense when Louise talked me through it, I had never made the explicit connection between the state of my mind in each domain being connected. It all starts at home.

The second lesson (and there were many more after that first chat) is the importance of gratitude. She taught me a simple practice. When you wake up in the morning, the first thing you should do as soon as you can is to find your cosy corner with your favourite hot beverage and write in your journal ten things you are grateful for. Once you have written them out, say each one aloud. After you finish reading out the first one, say thank you. Repeat twice. Go down on your list of ten. When I first understood how this was to be done, I cringed. Do I really need to say thank you thrice for everything I am grateful for. It felt new age and hokey. She asked me to trust her and try this practice consistently for a few months. She shared examples of how this practice has helped her and many of her clients.

I took a leap of faith in Louis's belief in gratitude and followed suit. I picked out a nice leather-bound diary I had in my collection and got to work. The first few days were quite easy. I had a long list of things to be grateful for. The unconditional love of my family. My work that gives me purpose and meaning. My friendships. My health. My home. I could even write more than ten. After a few days, it started getting tougher to write something different. When I was in a not-so-great mood, I found it difficult to be grateful for anything at all. But the instructions were to write every day without fail. It was OK to repeat things I am grateful for.

Like in many other areas of my life, I was disciplined in embracing gratitude in my life. I wrote in my gratitude journal consistently for many months. I kept reminding myself of how much good I had in my life, which was in stark contrast to what was happening because of Covid-19 in every country around the world including ours. Putting this in perspective helped me snap out of my self-absorption.

Slowly, I could start to see the difference in my daily life. I was more positive during the day and less irritable. The most mundane and inconsequential of things didn't get to me. I looked at my husband with more appreciation than I was used to doing. I spent more quality time with my parents knowing well that they were ageing and needed me more. At work, I focused on the strengths of my colleagues rather than on the things they could not do well. In short, writing in my journal every day changed my mental state from one of scarcity to one of abundance by focusing on the positives in every situation.

While it may seem like being thankful for even the smallest things may be the most difficult thing to do when you are feeling very down and hopeless, it is exactly the thing to do. Victor Frankl, author of *Man's Search for Meaning* concluded that 'the meaning of life is found in every moment of living'. The best way to deal with life's challenges is to take it moment to moment. Start with being thankful for what there is even if it means just being thankful for being alive.

I have taught this practice to my daughters and many colleagues at work. Teenagers can get into the mode of whining all the time. Once when my elder daughter was moaning, I forced her to sit down quietly and, on a blank sheet of paper, write down everything she was grateful for. She didn't like doing it and hemmed and hawed throughout, but I do think it opened her eyes to a different way of thinking and being.

In our race to achieve more and be successful, we can easily forget the things that help us be our best selves. It is important to acknowledge and remind yourself of these things every day. It will help you keep your feet firmly planted on the ground.

Your practice of gratefulness as a way of living should also spill over into the way you treat people. Always saying please and thank you is something so basic but many busy working adults seem to forget this. Yet, they are hygienic in building strong relationships. Even when you get feedback that may be negative, can you be the person who thanks the other for the feedback because surely it may help you?

Thank you. Two simple words that have the great power to influence outcomes in your life. Don't be stingy with these words. Say them often. Mean it sincerely. Live life every day with immense gratitude for everything you have.

Empathy

Empathy is not a word that I engaged with until I was well into my forties. Of course, I knew of it but it wasn't a part of my consciousness the way it is now.

At a basic level, empathy is about putting yourself in another person's shoes and trying to understand their perspective and point of view. Easy, right? Actually, it is more difficult than it sounds. Some people find it downright impossible to understand where someone else may be coming from.

Empathy is not to be confused with sympathy, though they are often used interchangeably. They are not the same thing. When your mother tells you how she's had a migraine for weeks on end, listening to her patiently and giving her care and love demonstrates sympathy. Empathy is trying to understand what she might be experiencing and to relate with her based on that understanding.

Women are generally thought to be more empathetic than men. Perhaps this is the reason why our workplaces are not very empathetic places. The primary job of managers is the welfare of their staff. The problem is that managers tend to be self-absorbed in making a mark themselves and achieving their goals. There is little time for empathy. MBA schools did not traditionally emphasise the importance of empathy. Even in our early schooling systems, the emphasis is much more on the individual rather than how we relate with others.

Things are changing. Design thinking, which has become hugely popular in the last decade, has firmly put the word 'empathy' in boardrooms. If you don't empathise with your customers, you drastically reduce the chances of creating products and services that they will love. There is a sea of sameness in almost every consumer category and consumers have plenty of choice.

You must be both relevant and different to stand out as a brand of choice with your customers. This means you must understand them deeply. This is where empathy comes in. An often-cited example is that of CavinKare in India. They understood that consumers in rural India could not afford the shampoos, oils and other products the company offered. Yet, they aspired to buy them. So, CavinKare innovated in pack size and created the now famous 'sachets' which allowed a sampling of the product at a fraction of the cost. And rural consumers got hooked. This could not have happened had the company not empathised with the aspirations of rural consumers. They might have just ignored the market thinking their products were not affordable to this consumer segment. Empathy unlocked this market opportunity.

Things are also changing with the role of Human Resources at companies. There is much more of an emphasis on people-centricity at organisations, especially post-Covid-19. Companies are now hugely empathetic to the 'whole life' challenges of their employees and are bending over backwards to retain their most talented employees by offering flexible working, an array of benefits and a much more empathetic approach to employee relations.

As someone who is keen to advance her career, you need to embrace empathy as it can propel your career.

How can you embrace more empathy to advance your career?

Shift from me to we. A big shift to make in the workplace is a team mindset. At school and at college it was all about you, your marks and your achievements. Nothing else mattered. This is a recipe for disaster at the workplace. The sooner you embrace a team mindset and lead with 'we', the sooner you will get acceptance and traction at the workplace. Companies are littered with 'me' types, which create toxicity for all others. You can set yourself apart and build your relationships by taking the opposite approach. It doesn't mean you are not focused on your goals and are not hungry for advancement. It's just that the way you do it is by working together and uplifting your peers rather than by trampling over them.

Listen intently. The gateway to empathy is to listen with your full attention. If there is one skill you must master that will help you immensely with all aspects of work, it is this. Talk less. Listen more. Listen for the spoken and the unspoken. Ask open-ended questions using 'what' and 'how'. Don't put others on the defensive by asking pointed 'why' questions. Don't interrupt. Let the other person speak to their heart's content. Don't be afraid of silence. Accept the awkward silences and let the other person fill the gaps. They will. Paraphrase what you have heard to make the other person feel understood. Don't be distracted while listening. Put your phone away. Use your facial gestures to signal empathy.

Become a people-centric manager. Many high achievers are great at meeting business goals. Often, this comes at the cost of driving their teams to burnout. You have an opportunity to be the manager who puts people first. Take the time to get to know your colleagues on a personal level. What are their aspirations? What are their anxieties? Who are they outside of work? What is the best way to collaborate with them and to manage or lead them?

Read more fiction. One of the best ways to become more empathetic is to read fiction. When you lose yourself in different worlds and get into the lives of complicated characters, your perspective changes. You start to understand and appreciate the full spectrum of human emotions. You get a deeper understanding of people's motivations. All this nurtures your own emotions as well, making you far more empathetic in real life. You can relate to different people better. You will be more sensitive to situations and have a greater appreciation for why people may do the things they do which may not seem logical to you.

Empathy is a force for good. Like with other skills, practice develops this muscle. It is not the most obvious of skills to invest in. Returns may not be immediate but the compounding of your empathetic approach over time is sure to give you a distinctive edge in your career.

Emotional Intelligence

'Emotional intelligence, more than any other factor, more than IQ or expertise, accounts for 85 per cent to 90 per cent of success at work. IQ is a threshold competence. You need it but it does not make you a star. Emotional intelligence can,' says Warren Bennis.

While college might be able to nurture our IQ, nobody guides us on emotional intelligence (EI). There are online courses offered by LinkedIn Learning, Udemy, etc., which explain to you the benefits of emotional intelligence and how to develop it. The best way is to learn by practising it at the workplace.

The best definition I have read is that emotional intelligence is the ability to manage your own emotions and to understand the emotions of people around you. It is not about being a nice person. Neither is it about being emotional or weak.

There have been several instances in my life where I learned the hard way that it was important for me to develop this capability.

As you read earlier, when I was working at Landor's London office, I was removed from a project and I didn't understand why. I cried uncontrollably when the managing director (MD) told me of the decision. I could not accept it. She hadn't given me particularly convincing reasons, but I made it worse by being in denial. That drama caused a lot of damage to the MD's perception of me, which prevented her from choosing me for plum opportunities later down the line. In hindsight, I could have handled this incident much more maturely. Little did I realise the impact it would have on my career.

Many years later, I had a big ego clash with a client over something very silly. We had a strong relationship with the client's father-in-law, who was the chairman of the company. Our client wanted to change the brand. He dug his heels in. I took the opposite position of protecting the brand, which is what I believed the chairman would have wanted to do. We were fired from the account because I was not emotionally intelligent enough to know when to back off.

The most important part about developing EI is knowing what's happening with your emotions. Can you pull yourself out of the situation metaphorically and observe what's going on? Can you then label the emotions to help build self-awareness? Research shows that when you increase your ability to name what you feel with a wide emotional vocabulary, your ability to regulate your emotions increases. I should, for example, have recognised I was engaging in an ego battle with a client and alarm bells should have rung sooner than they did. That would have given me an opportunity to backtrack and apologise before we were fired.

Being aware and regulating your emotions is half the job done. But EI will also help increase your empathy for others. As you develop the skill of seeing your own emotions through a different lens, you will also improve your ability to read the emotions of others, therefore becoming better at being more empathetic.

EI is most helpful when it comes to maintaining and strengthening relationships. In the past, when I did not share my emotions clearly or just brushed them under the carpet, there was a clear negative impact on relationships. What EI allows us to do is to communicate our needs honestly and clearly.

What are some ways of improving emotional intelligence?

Journal, especially at the end of the day, about three emotions you felt during the day. They could be positive emotions or negative emotions. It's important to write down how they impacted you. I do gratitude journaling in the morning and reflective journaling in the evening. Writing down and contemplating how things made you feel is valuable in improving your understanding of how you experience emotions and how you tend to react to them.

Develop empathy. It's good practice to look around and gauge how your co-workers may be feeling at any given moment. Is someone stressed? Another tired? A third just plain bored? Train yourself to read the emotions of others. Going up to them later and having a non-threatening conversation about what you observed can make your bond stronger. If I am intentionally putting myself in others' shoes, I'm naturally going to be more open and understanding of where they are coming from.

Practise active listening. Listening is a highly underrated skill in the workplace. So many of us are busy talking that we aren't really listening. If we were, we would be picking up insightful cues from what others are saying and not saying. Whenever I play back to others what I have heard from them or take notes, I notice the other person feeling happy that I am giving them respect, time and attention. Being fully present and not allowing distractions to interrupt the space you have created with the other person is critical.

Communicating clearly and effectively are important ways of improving EI. Writing and speaking well are foundational skills for career growth and help in communication. Don't remain locked up in your ivory tower. Stay connected by interacting with others as often as possible.

Stay positive. We all get bogged down by the emotional baggage we are carrying, but those who have high EI know that staying positive is the need of the hour, especially in situations where others may be stressed. Focus on how you might lift the mood or infuse energy with your positivity. Practising this skill as often as possible will make it a natural mode of operation for you, as it did for me.

Be open-minded. Curiosity crowds out judgement. One of my former bosses taught me the value of being open to new ideas and new perspectives from newcomers to our organisation. The more openness you demonstrate, the more easily people will approach you as they will see you as someone open to new ways of doing things.

Giving and receiving feedback is an art. The mechanism of feedback is an important one for improving emotional intelligence. Giving feedback may sound easier than receiving feedback, but it is trickier. Start with something positive to put the other person in a receiving mode. Remember to criticise the action or the work, not the person. Explain the impact of that action or low-quality work. Offer a suggestion or two on how the feedback may be addressed and don't leave the recipient hanging. I learned that when you are giving someone a dose of negative feedback, you must pad it with seven doses of positive feedback. Colleagues are like children – they don't like getting told off.

Receiving feedback is not that much easier. You must listen fully without being tempted to jump in. There's no room for defensiveness. Be fully present and absorb every word and feeling of what's being communicated to you. Play back what you heard. Make sure that you validate the words of the feedback giver. Ask if they have anything to add. The best thing you can say at the end is 'Thank you. I will consider your feedback.'

Stay calm no matter what. Tensions escalate. Emotions run wild. Can you be the one who is calm in the chaos? That's what highly emotionally intelligent people demonstrate. They don't crack under pressure. They may be nervous or worried on the inside, but they remain stoic outside. Deep breathing, writing things down, speaking calmly to a few trusted aides are all ways in which you can stay coolheaded.

Most rising stars underestimate the value of developing emotional intelligence. Have a plan for practising and improving your EI one day at a time.

Personal Relationships

A lot of happiness in life can be traced to the quality of your relationships. So important is our sense of connection to others that loneliness literally kills. Research has shown that those who are isolated and cut off from society have higher chances of dying earlier. A shocking study shows that social isolation is as damaging as smoking fifteen cigarettes a day or having six drinks a day. Loneliness increases the risk of heart disease and stroke by 30 per cent. Chronic loneliness can increase the risk of dementia by 50 per cent.

Why should you be worried? There's a slim chance that you are socially isolated and don't have close relationships with your family and friends. But there is a high chance that on the treadmill of work in the pursuit of success, you may neglect relationships. You may not give them the time and attention they deserve. The little-by-little neglect every week, every month may give way to fissures that will be harder to repair later on in life.

As you get busy with your career, your parents will start to age. There will be a role reversal and you will have to look after them in their old age the way they looked after you when you were a baby, a toddler and a teen. Don't make the mistake of neglecting your parents because work keeps you too busy. You'll need to make the extra effort to call them regularly and spend quality time with them. Many working professionals have this realisation only after their parents have passed away and wish they had spent less time at work and more time with their family.

While good relationships are nurturing for the soul, toxic relationships can be as damaging as loneliness. *My Cancer is Me* by Vijay Bhatt is an eye-opening book about the lifestyle factors that contribute to cancer. Toxic relationships are one of them. Our bodies absorb the pain and hurt of relationships gone wrong which can weaken our immune system and trigger our cancer genes. Therapy and self-work are some of the ways in which you can begin to heal yourself.

Speaking of self-work, we may not realise that many of us are in three marriages: one with our spouse/partner, one with our work/career and one with ourselves. The last one is equally if not more important than the others. David Whyte has written a deeply profound book on the integration of work, relationships and the inner selves called *The Three Marriages: Reimagining Work, Self and Relationship*.

This was one of my book club's reads a few years ago. It gave me a wake-up call on how little time I spent with myself. I had no rituals to nurture my self-relationship. This can be problematic. As David says, 'Neglecting this internal marriage, we can easily make ourselves a hostage to the externals of work and the demands of a relationship. We find ourselves unable to move in these outer marriages because we have no inner foundation from which to step out with a firm persuasion. It is as if, absent a loving relationship with this inner representation of our self, we fling ourselves in all directions in our outer lives, looking for love in all the wrong places.'

So while spending time with family and friends may be obvious, spending time with yourself is not so obvious. It came to me as a surprise that such a concept even exists. But when I thought about it, this is what the ancient sages did by meditating. They were spending time in their inner worlds. When you are at peace with yourself, the way you interact with the outer world is starkly different. You don't have to meditate to be with yourself. Sometimes, it can just be about sitting on your comfortable couch and enjoying your own company. No TV. No book. No cat or dog. No phone. Just you and your thoughts. My therapist taught me the importance of this practice. Enjoying your own company is an important skill to be mastered. I have written more about the art of silence in the earlier section on the Mind.

What are a few ways to deepen your relationship with yourself?

Schedule solo dates at least once a week. Sometimes it could be doing nothing. Other times it could be going alone to a movie, a restaurant or a museum. The important part is to treat this date as sacrosanct. Just as you would not let down a friend and cancel last minute, don't stand yourself up!

Practise journalling. When you reflect on how the day was, you develop a richer understanding of your daily behaviours. This self-awareness is an important part of knowing yourself more deeply.

Meditate regularly. The biggest benefit of meditating every day is that it makes you less reactive and more responsive to the environment. You become kinder and gentler to yourself and therefore to others.

Professional Relationships

Porter Gale, entrepreneur and public speaker, said, 'Your network is your net worth.'

I have seen this played out time and again in my life. Many people ask me how I get the opportunities I do. How did I get to be on the Cannes Lions Design Jury? How did I get invited to teach a course at BITS School of Management (BITSoM), a leading business school in India? How did I get to star in a Zoya brand campaign?

While the obvious answer is that I have a strong personal brand, the not-so-obvious answer is that it's all about my network.

You can have a broad and deep network as well. You just have to be systematic about how you meet people, develop relationships and keep nurturing the relationships, any of which may bring you the most phenomenal life-changing opportunities.

Infuse every new meeting with warmth

You don't have to go to networking events to build a network. If you have a busy working life, chances are you meet many people every week, every month. Think about the ones you remember the most. Likely, there was a lot of warmth when you met them. Remember what Maya Angelou said, 'I have learned that people will forget what you said, people will forget what you did, but people will never forget how you made them feel.'

Can you be the person infusing warmth into the interaction every time you meet someone? How do you create an unforgettable and incredibly warm first impression? Be present. Look for shared connections or hobbies. Smile. Be genuinely happy to have met the other person. When you are out at events, make the effort to meet as many people as you can. Quality matters because you must make every connection count.

Exchange contact information

When you meet someone you really connect with, the exchange of contact information happens without effort because both parties want to stay in touch. What you should do is also make it a point to get the information of even those you may not have initially had an immediate connection with. With LinkedIn and other social media platforms, it's easy. Make sure you send invites to everyone you meet. This is especially true in larger online or physical meetings. I make it a point to write down all the names so I can connect with them on LinkedIn later.

Get into give mode

The number one mistake a lot of people make is they immediately ask a new contact for a favour. The response is bound to be disappointing. What you should focus on is how you can add value to that new connection. Try to recall any shared interests or think of something that might be helpful to them. An article, a book recommendation, a link to a podcast or an offer to connect them to someone you know are some ways to establish yourself as a giver in the relationship.

Develop a system

The first couple of exchanges might be straightforward. The big difference is in how much effort you make to keep it going. Some may be online relationships only. Others you may make time for once in a while to meet for a coffee or a meal.

Keith Ferrazzi, author of the best-selling book *Never Eat Alone,* believes it's not what you know but who you know that matters. This is a must-read if you wish to actively build and nurture your network. The book is full of tips and techniques that will make an immediate difference to your approach.

One of my biggest takeaways from the book is to have a spreadsheet of all my key professional contacts and to track how often I am in touch with them.

Choose seven a week

One easy way to keep making progress with your network development goals is to randomly pick seven people from your network whom you are going to be in touch with in the coming week. It should not be people who you are already in regular touch with but those you have not connected with in a while (longer than three months). Flip through the contacts on your phone, go through your emails or look on LinkedIn, X or Instagram. Pick seven at random. And then mix it up.

You can choose to meet one contact in person. Another two, you may schedule calls with. The remaining four you could send a short note with a link to something useful or just pop in to say hello and that you were thinking of them. Your goal of warming seven connections a week is one way to be more intentional with how you consume social media. Rather than passively scrolling, think of how you might convert posts by your contacts into a reason for connection. Wish them on their birthday, congratulate them on their achievement, offer to help connect them to someone who might help.

The power of compounding

Develop this systematic approach of watering your network and patiently wait for the rewards to start coming in. You remember how compound interest works, right? It will all add up – trust the process. I vouch for it!

You'll also be surprised how sometimes the weakest links in your network bring you the best opportunities. So don't over-index on just the most important or powerful people. Treat each one as VIP because you never really know what gift they might bring you in the future.

Cultivating Joy

In my mid-forties, I had reached a point of mindless living from moment to moment on the treadmill of life. I usually had the energy to get through the day (though on some days it was very hard by the time evening came around) but when I look back, I wonder if I had truly enjoyed and relished any of the experiences I had, whether it was my daughter's milestone birthday, a promotion at work, a special gift received from a dear friend or just quality time with close family and friends. I was busy moving from one thing to the next, not to mention the endless worrying, stress and despair I felt along the way. This was also at the height of the Covid-19 pandemic, which was creating havoc all around.

In that accelerated, dizzy and blurring-of-boundaries pace of life, I had forgotten what it meant to stop and smell the roses. I felt disconnected from others and myself. I didn't really want to do anything other than work, sleep and rest. Reading was my only succour.

The joy was sucked out from my daily life. Nothing moved me emotionally. It was not a good place to be. Even reading did not give me the joy it used to before.

Ingrid Fettel Lee's *Joyful: The Surprising Power of Ordinary Things to Create Extraordinary Happiness* first brought me awareness of the importance of truly savouring moments throughout the day.

Ingrid's book inspired me to create a challenge for myself to find joy. For thirty days, fifteen minutes after lunch every day, I walked around in my neighbourhood actively appreciating nature. It was a scavenger hunt for joy, if you will! I can't tell you how much I started to enjoy these walks after the first few days. With every passing day, I found my numbness slowly receding to the background. I started feeling a variety of emotions again. This challenge got me out of my head and into my body.

Inspired by Ingrid's blog 'The Aesthetics of Joy', I documented my own #aestheticsofjoy campaign on Instagram as a way of reminding myself how easy it was to consciously connect with the world to find delight in the simplest of things whether that is a rose blooming in the garden or a genuine smile from a stranger. This simple exercise set me on a path of being more mindful about bringing joy into my every day.

A year later, I was delighted to learn about Ingrid's seven-day self-guided online course, 'The Joy Jumpstart'. I signed up for it to further embed joy deeply in my being. Here are the lesson goals for each of the seven days.

Day 1: Find the sparks

Day 2: Tune your senses

Day 3: Map your joyful world

Day 4: Live in the now

Day 5: Envision your joyful life

Day 6: Make space for joy

Day 7: Plan for joy

An email is sent to you every day from which you download a worksheet that you can work through at your own pace.

It's a very well-thought through, experiential course that I loved.

It taught me to be more in tune with myself and therefore find more joy in my everyday life, which then manifests in the form of inner well-being and peace.

While I highly recommend the course, you don't have to go through it to start to cultivate more joy. Just decide you will take on the mindset of looking for joy in the most unexpected places. Perhaps start with a documenting project like I did. Suddenly all your senses will be switched on and the magic of joy will fill you up.

Leading a Psychologically Rich Life

Eleanor Roosevelt believed that 'the purpose of life is to live it, to taste experience to the utmost, to reach out eagerly without fear for newer and richer experience.'

There is a new dimension of the good life that has been increasingly getting research attention: psychological richness. A psychologically rich life is one in which we collect a broad range of interesting experiences during which we engage the mind and feel deep emotions – both positive and negative. If you want to pursue this route to a good life, then you must start thinking about how to get more novelty, variety, complexity, intensity, depth and surprise in your daily life.

This is a different kind of life compared to the two more popular ones: a happy life and a meaningful life. A happy life is defined by hedonistic living. You live primarily to enjoy pleasures. A meaningful life on the other hand is characterised by purpose, meaning, service and sacrifice.

A psychologically rich life involves complex mental engagement. Sometimes the emotions will be pleasant, sometimes not. The objective is to keep looking for ways to expose your mind to the broad spectrum of emotions that come from varied experiences.

So why should you pursue it? It won't necessarily give you happiness or money, but it will ensure that you are rarely bored. Leading such a life will make you more open, more curious and more creative, all of which bodes well for whatever it is you wish to achieve. When you step outside the routine regularly, you bring back something to your daily life which is enriching. It could be travelling to an unknown destination, a night out at a restaurant you don't usually dine at, watching a play or meeting new friends at an event – these are all the types of experiences you can consciously gather.

As your professional life gets busy, it's tempting to focus all your energy on work. I see young professionals become workaholics within a few years of entering the workplace. Work becomes their primary identity. They are so stressed about doing a good job at work that they are willing to sacrifice everything else. But all work and no play makes Jane a dull girl, right? I have seen that these workaholics are ironically the least interesting people on a team. They don't have passions or experiences to tap into to add richness to discussions. Their ideas may lack inspiration when compared to those who lead psychologically rich lives. If they carry on like this for a decade or longer, they may find themselves socially isolated. When I find myself tipping over into workaholic mode, I remember this and try to get my balance back.

Make sure you are going out, meeting friends, exercising and signing up for new activities. Do things that give you interesting new experiences. This is an excellent stage of life at which you inculcate practices to make yourself a lifelong learner. Learning should not stop after graduating from college and entering the workplace. You must constantly be up-skilling in areas of hard and soft skills to give yourself a competitive advantage.

Things get hard for working women who have children. If life has so far revolved around work, it then revolves around kids. Taking care of kids while fulfilling professional duties can be exhausting. I gave birth to two kids in two years. I know how little energy one has left for anything else. But this is precisely when you have to push yourself and do things for yourself outside of work and home to keep yourself mentally engaged.

I joined a book club, which was a nice excuse to force myself to make time for reading. The monthly get-togethers with the book club were a nice respite from the routine as well. These days young moms are going back to exercise much faster than usual. Maybe it's not Pilates for you. It could just be a walk around the block. Who knows who you may bump into leading to an interesting conversation. Make time for movie night. Go out and experience new things. It's important at this stage in your career to nurture your psychological richness to prevent yourself from falling into postpartum depression.

When your children have left home and you are an empty nester, it may be tempting to throw yourself fully into work. Here again, you should be careful not to become unidimensional. Take time out for friends and to try new experiences in your life. This life stage is big. Watch out because it can be tempting to give your all to work. I slip into that mode quite often. I have to remind myself that work is not life. Yes, I must toil hard to give my work my best, but it should not become the be-all and end-all of my existence. Don't neglect your parents either. Even if you don't live in the same city, make time to chat and engage in their lives. It means a lot to them, and it will help you in more ways than you imagine, making you a whole lot less self-centred and prone to wallowing in self-pity when things may not go right in the workplace. This is also a good time in your life to invest in learning new skills because you will have more time on your hands. Pick topics you want to learn more about (either related or unrelated to work) and ensure you set up a learning calendar to systematically tick off your learning goals.

How have I led a psychologically rich life?

Outside of work, I have a large network of professional and personal contacts that I meet regularly. I play tennis, swim, workout with a physical trainer and practice yoga. As a family, we invest in at least four holidays a year in both new and familiar places. Usually, we pack in adventure and sport and other times it's more of a cultural immersion. Over the years, I have tried golf, scuba diving and skiing to name a few. I am part of a non-fiction book club (and have been for four years) which exposes me to new ideas through the books we read. I spent a few years improving my Spanish skills but then gave it up to make time for more writing and dedicating time to my weekly newsletter, 'Ideas to Play With'. I also make occasional visits to museums, theatre performances or music shows all of which I'd like to indulge much more in.

What has living a psychologically rich life done for me and why should you consider it?

It has made me much more creative. My diverse experiences are a boon when I am in brainstorming mode. Ideas come to me from everywhere. I am rarely stuck staring at a blank page and praying for an idea to magically appear.

It has made me more emotionally resilient. I have experienced a broader range of emotions that I can fall back on during times of stress. When I am nervous about a client meeting, I remind myself how I conquered my fear of scuba diving and this was going to be easy-peasy.

By trying so many different things, I have a better understanding of myself. I know what I like, what I don't like, what energises me, what drains me. This self-awareness helps me make better choices in my life.

I have better relationships across the board. I am less self-centric and more empathetic. I can also contribute more to other people because of my life experiences. I find myself being a calmer, kinder and more compassionate person.

Most importantly, these diverse and rich experiences have made me a more positive person whom others find inspiring.

When you live through fulfilling life experiences, you will find a wonderfully magical way of uplifting others.

Authenticity and Vulnerability

'Just be yourself' – we hear this often. But how easy is it in practice?

I wish someone had drilled the importance of authenticity into my head when I was much younger. I went through so many years of my teens and twenties trying to fit in. This is primarily because I had to switch schools and colleges often. From Baldwin Girls to The Valley School, Queen Mary's to Cathedral and John Connon, Davidson to SP Jain Institute of Management and Research, changing cities, changing countries. When you join a new school all you want to do is to blend in and not stand out. You want to fit in and be accepted. Especially when you are in a foreign country, you feel the right thing to do is to assimilate and not stand out like a sore thumb. Thus, from an early age, I was pre-programmed not to value my authentic self.

During my first job at Ogilvy in Mumbai, I was worried my colleagues might not approve of my sartorial choices. I feared they would mock my taste in music. I suspected they may be talking behind my back and mocking my accent because I was a 'foreign return.' I had studied abroad for my undergrad and had come back to India to work. I was filled with anxieties. These same fears were magnified when I started at Landor in San Francisco as it was a completely different culture. It was just exhausting to constantly worry about what others were thinking and to manage myself accordingly.

When this mindset carries with you into the world of work, it can be a huge disadvantage. When you are floating in the sea of sameness, you risk not being noticed because you sound like and look like everyone else. You may dress a certain way to fit in. You may speak a certain way because that's what you think is required. When you are not true to yourself or who you are, you risk being seen as fake. One of our creative directors in London once told me frankly that he felt I was sharing with him things about me that I felt he wanted to hear. He told me to stop that and share my real interests, my true motivations and my naked ambitions without putting a spin on everything. That gave me permission to talk from my heart and the floodgates opened. My relationship with that creative director changed dramatically and I could see how we then started having a very different kind of bond.

It wasn't well into mid-career that I started having confidence in who I am, my identity (as a global Indian), my likes, my dislikes and my point of view on anything and everything. It wasn't a particular instance that made me suddenly wake up one day to embrace authenticity, but it gradually happened as I started seeing that people were interested in unique aspects of me and my personality. Fitting in with others made me less interesting.

I also realised that our clients, especially the more senior and experienced ones, value those who dare to disagree, who have conviction in their ideas and who are unafraid of seniority. This realisation made me more confident of being authentic.

When I look back, I wish I had the courage to be authentic from the time I started my career. Who knows, I may have made more interesting friends, and my career might have even taken a different path.

What should you do to embrace authenticity as a way of being at work?

Know yourself. You must do the self-work to understand your aspirations as well as your anxieties. Self-awareness is the foundation of authenticity.

Be honest. Say what's in your heart. Don't sugar-coat things. Don't say what you think others want to say. Don't shy away from saying anything at all. Learn to always express your opinion in the most professional way possible.

Be vulnerable. It's OK to open yourself to criticism. Develop a thick skin. Admit your mistakes. Don't be afraid to ask for help. It's OK to not be a know-it-all. In fact, know-it-alls can be highly annoying in workplaces. We're all human. We're all imperfect. Imperfection adds an interesting dimension to your personality.

Be fearless. You must let go of the doomsday scenarios for any act of authenticity you may be contemplating. Just let go. The consequences are usually far less severe than your mind may be conjuring.

Be respectful. When you express your honest opinion, you are likely to offend others but don't offend with the goal of offending. It's OK to disagree, but remember to be always respectful and professional.

Be patient. It's not easy to be authentic from the get-go. You'll slowly practise and get better at being more authentic. You may feel bad initially because you may get laughed at or face backlash when you express your real opinions. It's OK. Don't get overly affected emotionally. Stay calm and the situation will tide through. Be kind to yourself and stay on the path of authenticity. Patience will help you get better and better.

Lack of authenticity is exacerbated for leaders who may adopt a leadership style that does not fit in with their values, as this can be recognised by others immediately. Lack of authenticity is the number one reason your team may not be connected to you. Your clients may not truly value you because they will sense you are saying things you want them to hear. I learned this the hard way when some clients pushed me to share my true opinion on what decision they should take.

One client, in particular, taught me how to always give my opinion by saying, 'If it were my decision …' or 'If it were my business …' This forced me to develop my own point of view in every situation and to be more authentic. I must admit it was not easy. I was always afraid I might give the wrong answer, but I had to get over the fear. Now I am prepared with my answer and the logic of how I arrived at it without worrying too much about how I will be perceived because I answered in a certain way. That's the fear that we must get rid of. We must not live every day worrying about how we will be perceived because that fear drives us to act and speak in ways that may not be genuine.

Now let's talk about vulnerability. It's a term that has crept into the discourse of leadership in the last decade. It is one of those loosely bandied around corporate terms that has become fashionable, yet nobody quite knows what it is or rather has their own interpretation of it. For me, vulnerability is closely linked to authenticity. I define it as the courage to be your true self, to act and speak the way that comes naturally to you, to speak the truth, to not be afraid to make mistakes, to own up for mistakes made and to develop a thick skin toward criticism because you will invariably get heaps of it when you are not pandering to what others want to hear. It's also about asking for help when you need it either in terms of the skills you need to learn or the mentorship you need to grow.

Being vulnerable does not mean being disrespectful or trampling over others' feelings or not caring what others think. It calls for heightened sensitivity, empathy and emotional intelligence to navigate every situation.

As you rise in the organisation, it is easy to think you are infallible and can do no wrong. When hubris sets in, it can be the beginning of the end. This is why authenticity and vulnerability help you stay grounded and real. This is what your teams and customers want.

Those of us who are people pleasers may find it particularly challenging to be authentic and vulnerable. We are so focused on pleasing others that we don't summon the courage to say or do anything that can cause pain to us. In the long term, this is a no-win situation for both parties.

To dig deeper into the topic of vulnerability, I would recommend Brene Brown's *The Power of Vulnerability*. Her book emphasises the importance of building genuine connections and resilience.

Here are some key things to keep in mind:

Embrace imperfections. Accept yourself as you are, imperfections and all. It's OK not to have all the answers or to make mistakes; vulnerability fosters self-acceptance.

Choose courage over comfort. Embrace discomfort and have the courage to speak up, share your ideas and confront challenges. This bravery fosters personal and professional growth.

Authenticity builds trust. Be genuine and authentic in your interactions. Authenticity creates trust and fosters meaningful relationships with colleagues and superiors.

Seek support. Don't be afraid to ask for help or lean on others. Vulnerability allows you to seek support when needed, leading to collaborative solutions and personal well-being.

Build resilience through vulnerability. Vulnerability is not a weakness but a source of resilience. Being open about challenges and failures enables you to bounce back stronger and learn from setbacks.

Cultivate empathy. Understand others' perspectives and be empathetic toward their vulnerabilities. This fosters a supportive work environment where everyone feels valued and understood.

Be a 'Lovecat'

When you were entering the world of work for the first time, you may have been advised to not feel bad about selling your soul to the big, bad corporate world of capitalism, a world where aggression, predatory behaviour, greed, rudeness, dishonesty and other bad actions may be commonplace. You may have been prepared to fight this with your own brand of defence, thinking that this was just par for the course, and you had to also learn to be this way as you grew in the organisation.

What I want to tell you is that things are changing rapidly. As Tim Sanders (a former senior executive at Yahoo) had introduced to the world in 2002, love can be a powerful force in business, and by becoming a 'lovecat' you can stand out, create positive relationships and propel your growth.

People who don't embrace love and kindness in today's workplace will lose out. There are two primary reasons for this.

The first reason is that we have an abundance of choice in every area. Pertaining to careers, we don't have to work for companies with toxic cultures. We also have a choice to walk away from bosses with toxic behaviours. If you lead a company that has a bad culture or you don't have the traits of a good leader, you will lose people.

The second reason is that bad behaviours are easily exposed in an era of transparency, thanks to the popularity and ubiquity of social media platforms. Insensitive comments, gross misconduct, bullying – these behaviours can be your downfall. All it would take is one tweet or post to bring you down no matter how unfounded.

So can you take the personal definition of love defined by Milton Mayerly as 'the selfless promotion of the other' and turn it into a business definition of love, defined by Tim Sanders as 'the act of intelligently and sensibly sharing knowledge, networks and compassion with your business partners'?

If you fully embody three characteristics – knowledge, network and compassion – you can become a full-fledged lovecat whose potential for growth becomes limitless.

If there's only one advice I wish I had been given when I was entering the world of work, it would have been this one: to be more of a lovecat! Being a lovecat will make a positive difference to the way you are perceived and therefore your opportunities for growth.

Let's break each characteristic down.

Knowledge

Be the person who knows the most. Read voraciously. Not just magazines and blogs but in-depth books in the areas of your expertise and other general topics. The trick to reading and accumulating knowledge as I have discussed in other parts of the book is finding a way to digest it and use it so it's retained in your brain.

I learned a simple formula from Tim Sanders on this: EPA.

Encode: Spend the time and energy to truly understand the material deeply and not just at surface level. Read many times if you have to. Look up words. Keep a list of new words you are learning. My girls joke about this, but it has helped me expand my vocabulary manyfold over the years.

Process: Underline, highlight and write notes. Do whatever it takes to process what you are reading in a form that is relevant to you. Find a way to organise the insights so you can access them later. For physical books, I write notes on the sides, underline and mark key points and summarise the core at the end of each chapter and at the end of the book overall. When I read online, I put key points in a note in the Notes app on my phone.

Apply: This is where the spark is ignited. Without this step, it's just information, not applied knowledge. Share it with someone. Say it out loud to a colleague. Use it in your writing. Practice the ritual. Anything that will take the knowledge off the page and into the real world so it can add value for you.

The most important aspect of creating value with knowledge is sharing with your network. Practice generosity in its truest sense. You are not giving away your edge by sharing knowledge with others. Paradoxically, you create an edge when you share your expertise.

Network

This is another topic I have discussed in the book. In the context of being a lovecat, the guidance is to build as large and as deep a network as you can. And to keep the nodes warm by sharing your knowledge generously with your network. Pay attention to everyone, not only the most important or the most senior of the closest members of your network. In fact, research has shown that very often you get the best opportunities from weaker links in your network. Treat each person as potentially the MVP in your network. Practice kindness and generosity with them no matter what their place in the world is today.

Compassion

While you may have heard of the importance of gathering knowledge and building a network, it is unlikely that you have been asked to be loving and kind in the workplace. This third characteristic can make the difference in the way people perceive you. Be genuinely interested in people's lives. Listen to their spoken and unspoken needs. Find ways to truly empathise and hone in on how you can be compassionate towards them and make them feel good. This can truly be a game changer in your relationship. In a world where everyone is self-centred, your focus on the other person will stand out and be appreciated. Consider all tools, from the tone of your voice, the warmth of your handshake, the genuineness of your smile to the lightness of your touch.

When you combine knowledge, network and compassion, you will develop into a charismatic and irresistible soul moulded in the archetype of the lovecat as Tim Sanders defined it. You will stand out from the pack. You will radiate love and positivity, which will attract the best people and opportunities. You will be liked and trusted more. All of this will advance you in the workplace.

Be Kind, Always

'Showing generosity and forgiveness even to those who do not deserve it is not weak but extraordinarily powerful.'

I can never forget this potent sentence from Julia Baird's *Phosphorescence*. Julia says that kindness should not just be an aspiration but a daily practice, a muscle that if exercised, can grow strong and become a habit or a way of life.

I love the idea of deploying kindness ubiquitously – in every situation and with every person – rather than hoarding it to be given out on special occasions for special people only.

How easily do we get irritated by people, things or circumstances! We allow these petty annoyances to take control of us and bring out our worst in the form of profanities, aggressive behaviour and emotional drama. I look back on my day, my week, my month, my year … and boy, am I guilty of operating at that low level on many, many occasions!

How might we channel our inner grace in every situation? How might we always think of what the other person may be going through before we are harsh and unkind towards them?

Maybe the taxi driver on the road who is honking loudly had a fight with his wife before he left home. Maybe the delivery boy who bumped into you in your apartment building's stairway is preoccupied with paying back the EMI on a mobile phone purchase. Maybe the middle-aged woman who elbowed past you in security at the airport is about to miss her flight to her father's funeral.

We will never be able to peek into the inner worlds of others to sense and feel their anxieties, but how do we learn to always give the other person the benefit of the doubt?

For a week, as I wrote this, I was extra conscious in every situation I encountered. I practised identifying and labelling situations when I could feel my irritation or impatience rising. Whenever I would sense myself starting to be judgemental of someone, I learned to red flag it and turn it into a moment of curiosity or care. Rather than pass a snap judgement or a harsh comment, I asked a question instead. Are you alright? Is something bothering you? Is everything OK at home?

My maid was making so many mistakes in the kitchen, it was driving me crazy, so when I asked her if everything was OK, I learned that her father had lost his job and overnight she had become the sole breadwinner of a family of seven. I stopped in my tracks. I was embarrassed by my behaviour.

A co-worker was exasperated. He just didn't know what to do in so many situations. When I asked why he was struggling he shared that nobody had taught him that there was a better way to do things. We had failed him, not the other way around.

Kindness is not about acts of charity performed occasionally to make yourself feel better as a human being. It is about acts of curiosity and acts of concern that you practise every day to ensure that how you deal with people at a fundamental level is by going through their door not yours.

Part 2

Promote Yourself

One of the most powerful tools in going further, faster in your career is your personal brand.

In Part 1 of the book, I shared my holistic approach to professional development, which involves the mind, the body and the soul. This lays the foundation and shapes your mindset.

You are now ready to think about how to articulate the value you bring to your organisation. You are ready to brand yourself.

In Part 2 of my book, I'm going to help you understand the basic concept of branding. Then we will talk about the origin and evolution of personal branding and the edge it can give you in today's highly competitive marketplace for talent. We will then discuss the common reasons why people don't invest in building their personal brands. By then I would have hopefully convinced you on why you should spend time and energy on your personal brand. We will look at all the advantages of personal branding and then you will be ready to deep dive into the 'how' of personal branding.

I've developed a process called the Five Acts of Personal Brand Building which I will take you through in detail. I was inspired by the Double Diamond Design Thinking Model, originally conceived by the Design Council in 2005, which has become a cornerstone of design thinking.

Act 1: Discover your personal brand

Act 2: Define your personal brand

Act 3: Design your personal brand

Act 4: Deploy your personal brand

Act 5: Deliver your personal brand

Personal branding is no longer a luxury but an essential element in the toolkit of every aspiring professional. The sooner you embrace the concept and start building your personal brand, the easier it will be for you to attract your prized opportunities.

Let's start by understanding the origin of the concept of a brand.

The word 'brand' comes from Old English, Old German and Norse words, all of which roughly translate as 'to burn' or 'fire'. People would mark their livestock by burning the animals' hides with a hot iron to indicate ownership. This practice of branding livestock spread from Egypt to Europe in ancient times, which is when it was assimilated into our present-day vocabulary.

With the advent of the Industrial Revolution and mass production, the need for differentiation of mass products became critical, which gave birth to modern-day packaging. Companies started using graphic design to create a unique identity for their products in a crowded marketplace. They trademarked their logos and packaging designs, which became a key tool in creating brand recognition and fostering loyalty. As early as 1837, Tiffany & Co. used a distinct colour on all its packs to signal quality and luxury. The Coca-Cola Company took the concept even further by developing a unique glass bottle design for its carbonated beverage brand, Coca-Cola, which lasts to this day.

As the advertising and branding industries developed to support the marketing of mass products, the concept of a brand evolved to become not just a marker of identity for companies but also a vehicle for emotional associations. Walter Landor, the founder of Landor, famously said, 'Products are manufactured in the factory, but brands are built in the mind.' Brands became a way in which companies could strengthen their relationships with their customers by evoking desires, emotions and other intangible attributes through their branding. A brand started to be seen as a promise that companies were making to their customers.

Today, a brand has become a multidimensional concept. It is no longer limited to a marker or a promise. Branding has evolved beyond products to services and experiences. It is also an experience that must be felt by customers at every touchpoint of the brand. The delivery of the brand is as important as the promise. If, for example, the Indigo brand stands for efficiency and a quirky sense of humour, then that must be felt in every interaction that the customer has with the brand, from the website where the ticket is booked to the check-in experience and the in-flight experience among the myriad other interaction points with the customer. Companies are also using the concept of brand to strengthen their relationships with employees and not just customers in the quest to attract and retain the best talent. This is the realm of employer branding.

David Aaker, a widely respected business consultant and author, was the first to help businesses understand the commercial value of a brand. He introduced the idea of brand equity and encouraged businesses to think of brands as assets that have long-term value for the business. Protecting, nurturing and developing brand equity to add value to the business is the task of modern-day brand management.

An important distinction has emerged between brand and branding. The brand is what you want to stand for in the eyes of your target audiences. Branding is all the signals you send via your logos, colours, communication, etc.

A brand is the identity of a business or product, encompassing a wide range of elements that collectively shape the perception of that business or product in the minds of consumers. These elements include the name of the product, service or company, the logo that represents the brand, a brand line encapsulating the brand's message, design elements such as colour schemes, typography and packaging and the reputation.

In essence, a brand is the holistic sum of how a product or business is perceived by its audience, incorporating both tangible and intangible elements.

Branding is the process and set of actions involved in creating, developing and managing a brand. This includes:

Creating Visual Elements: Designing logos, choosing colour palettes and developing other visual assets that represent the brand.

Defining Brand Voice: Establishing a consistent tone, style and messaging that aligns with the brand's identity and values.

Building Brand Awareness: Using marketing strategies to make the brand known to a wider audience, such as advertising campaigns, social media presence and public relations.

Maintaining Brand Consistency: Ensuring that all aspects of the brand are consistent across all platforms and interactions, which helps to build trust and loyalty among consumers.
Evolving the Brand: Adapting and updating the brand as needed to stay relevant and competitive in the market.

Branding is an ongoing process that aims to strengthen the brand's presence and ensure it resonates with its target audience.

Now let's shift our focus to personal branding, the most exciting development in the world of brands. The concept of personal branding was first popularised by Tom Peters, one of my favourite business authors, in an article by *Fast Company* in 1997 titled 'The Brand Called You' in which it was clear that everybody, not just celebrities or CEOs, needed to craft their image. This article is considered a seminal piece on self-advocacy in the workplace. Peters wrote, 'Regardless of age, regardless of position, regardless of the business we happen to be in, all of us need to understand the importance of branding. We are CEOs of our own companies. Me Inc. To be in business today, our most important job is to be head marketer for the brand called You.'

Tom Peters was the first to appropriate the concept of brand to individuals and state that just as companies develop brands to create differentiation in the marketplace, so too should individuals develop personal brands that can give them an edge and help advance their careers.

You cannot just hide behind your computer and expect the organisation to recognise your value. You must consciously promote yourself and create visibility for your personal brand. Your 'brand narrative' or the story you tell the world about yourself should be drawn from your unique strengths, skills and experiences. It is vital for you to find a way to not only discover your uniqueness but also consciously cultivate it in your career.

The key is authenticity. It is very important to create a personal brand true to who you are. Otherwise, it will end up damaging your prospects instead of helping them. People can detect disingenuity very easily. Tom Peters also touches upon the importance of building your network as a critical aspect of developing your personal brand. It is not a one-time exercise, but something that has to be continuously refined. Part of this journey is not just packaging yourself as you grow but also genuinely investing in learning and professional development, embracing change and taking risks.

He says, 'Today, in the Age of the Individual, you have to be your own brand. You're going to have to stand out to compete in today's world. You've got to stand for something. You've got to be special.'

The crux of personal branding is about deliberately choosing how you want to be remembered and what you want your legacy to be. Imbuing this in your personal brand, your most valuable asset, will reap you rich rewards.

Personal branding has become much easier in many ways since the time Tom Peters first introduced the concept in his *Fast Company* article. It has come into popularity in the recent few years due to the transformational impact of the internet and mobile revolutions. Round-the-clock social media has made building a personal brand easier and more fulfilling than ever.

However, the rampant misuse of the concept has led to scepticism about its value and even downright disgust at the crassness of self-promotion masquerading as personal branding.

Every time I've made a presentation on personal branding to a group of interested professionals, I've discovered a new barrier that people have, or yet, another challenge, in embracing the need to actively promote oneself. The list of barriers runs the gamut from the internal ('I hate the idea of being my own spokesperson') to the more external ('I don't have any money to invest in building a website for my personal brand').

There is a lot of enthusiasm for the idea of personal branding but very little energy for the act of personal branding. People seem to understand the importance but don't want to put in the effort that is required. Many don't think they have the discipline and consistency needed to build a personal brand.

Let's examine each of the barriers that you may face in building your personal brand and my responses to these doubts.

I am a human being, not a product or a service. I don't want to be packaged.

The very idea of using an approach that is used for corporate and product brands is anathema to some. There is a belief that the emotions, feelings, motivations and desires of humans are far too complex and nuanced for this approach.

A: You're right. It's far more difficult to pin down one unique strength of an individual than it is for a product or a service. However, the concept is powerful when there is a consistent story you tell about yourself (your strengths, your skills, your experiences) to the world. This helps you stand out and stand for something that people are drawn to. So rather than seeing only the complexities, think of personal branding as a tool to shine the light on what makes you unique and valuable.

Personal branding is not relevant to my career.

People who run their own businesses feel that the concept has no relevance for them as they must focus their energies on marketing and selling their products, not themselves.

A: This could not be further from the truth. Investors are buying into you as much if not more than into your idea for a business. The strength of the personal brand of the founder strongly correlates to the strength of the business.

Isn't personal branding only for celebrities?

Some feel it is worth the effort only for celebrities to invest in their personal brands as it is the source of their livelihoods but does not make sense for ordinary people.

A: While celebrities cannot afford to neglect to build and nurture their personal brands, the concept, if applied correctly, can be a path to growth and ample opportunities for any individual. Personal branding is not just for celebrities.

I don't want to come across as fake!

There is a genuine fear among many that anything they claim about themselves may be exaggerated and thus come across as not genuine.

A: The only way to counter this is to develop a meaning for your personal brand that is rooted in truths about who you are and what your special capabilities are.

My work should speak for itself.

Some people don't believe that talking about their achievements or trying to promote themselves in any manner whatsoever is ethical. They would rather just put their heads down and show up to work diligently.

A: The world is too competitive. If you don't create visibility for yourself and your work, it can and will often go unnoticed. Even your boss is too busy to think about you. You must take charge.

I'm afraid of coming across as a crass self-promoter.

One of the biggest barriers to personal branding is the risk of being judged by others as a narcissist and self-promoter. This is especially true if people believe that personal branding is all about social media promotion.

A: Yes, some people will think that no matter how authentically you approach personal branding. You just have to live with it. The simplest way is to ensure that you define your personal brand to focus on the value you create for others rather than on just your skills. For example, you could be the world's most experienced brand strategist, or you could be the world's most experienced brand strategist who helps brands find their unique North Star and profit from it. Which one will appeal more?

I am not social media savvy.

Related to the previous point, not being social media savvy is a barrier if you think that personal branding is all about having social media visibility.

A: You don't have to be on social media to have a personal brand. It's also about how you show up at work and how you interact with your colleagues and customers. Use social media if you want to reach out to more people and build new relationships with the hope of harvesting new and exciting opportunities in the future.

I worry about taking credit for team achievements.
Some people worry that all their work happens in the context of teams and that taking any credit for anything they work on will be doing a disservice to other members of the team.

A: You are right to worry about taking credit for a team's achievement. You can simply talk about this in the context of being part of the team. For example, you could position yourself as the key insight miner in the agency's A Team that creates award-winning work.

I don't like putting out so much information about myself in the public domain.
This is a limiting belief for those who think that personal branding is just about talking about your achievements on social media platforms like Facebook, Instagram and LinkedIn.

A: Again, you don't have to be on social media to have a personal brand. However, depending on your level of ambition, amplifying your brand using social media channels may or may not be right for you. Think this through because once you are on, you do have to share more about yourself to keep your personal brand relevant and differentiated. People are drawn to human stories and genuine experiences, which requires you to share more rather than less.

I don't have any money to build my personal brand.
Some people believe that anything to do with branding requires money. Hence not having money to invest in your personal brand is a significant barrier for many.

A: More than money, you need to set aside time and energy to build a personal brand. To amplify your personal brand on social media, a small budget may be required to, say, build a website or shoot professional photographs of yourself, but these are all well worth the investment.

For those just starting out and not wanting to invest at all, you could also look to your personal network for help. Perhaps you can find a friend or acquaintance with excellent photography skills or you can even barter your skills for others. There is always room to get creative with increasing the production quality of your personal brand assets.

I don't know what my real strengths are. How will I brand myself?
You may believe in the concept of personal branding, but then your limited understanding of yourself becomes a hindrance to doing something about your own brand.

A: Very true. A thorough awareness and understanding of yourself is an important first step in personal brand building. In Act 1, we will discuss different methods to discover your true strengths.

Self-promotion can be exhausting. I don't have the time or energy to build my personal brand.
There is a recognition that building your brand takes time, and many simply believe that they don't have the time or energy to take on such an endeavour.

A: There are no shortcuts. To build a strong personal brand you need to be deliberate about your approach, invest time and be consistent.

It takes a couple of years to get started and many more years of effort to polish and refine the structure. Like we've talked about earlier in the book, the power of compounding then takes over and you will have established a powerful personal brand in a seemingly short period of time.

Advantages of Having a Personal Brand

While you may be starting to buy into the concept of personal branding, let's look even more closely at why it's so important and the distinct advantages it can give you.

These are the three main challenges for brands to stand out today: sea of sameness, over communication and endless distractions.

For every job, there are thousands of applicants. This is not true only for jobs. Even supermarket shelves for products as basic as toothpaste have many brands fighting for the consumer's attention without offering much distinction. You can easily get lost in the sea of sameness.

As humans, we are also faced with over-communication in the urban societies we live in. I used to think that aeroplanes were one of the few places you would not be bombarded with commercial messages but even that has changed. Most airlines, especially the low-cost ones, are using the back of the seats to show brand advertising to consumers. Go to a public restroom and even there you may not escape an advertisement or hoarding! When we are faced an information overload we tune out.

Do you know that humans have an attention span of roughly eight seconds? It is less than that of a goldfish! Our attention keeps shifting from one thing to another. The pings of phones announcing the arrival of notifications do not help the cause. Endless distractions mean we aren't paying attention even when it matters the most, let alone insignificant matters. People are paying a lot less attention to us than we might imagine, so we must work that much harder to stand out.

In a society besieged by such mighty challenges to how human beings notice the world around them, it becomes extremely difficult to stand out, to get noticed, to be considered, to be preferred and to stay preferred. However, doing so is the route to getting the opportunities you want and getting them again and again and again.

Here is where having a personal brand can help immensely.

It establishes your niche. What are the keywords, associations and feelings you want to attach to your name? How do you want to set yourself apart? In a world of thousands of engineers, what kind of engineer are you? Author Todd Henry, for instance, has established a distinct niche. Positioning himself as 'an arms dealer for the creative revolution', he teaches organisations and individuals how to establish practices that lead to everyday brilliance.

It simplifies choice. A distinct personal brand can help you cut through the clutter. The story of twenty-one-year-old Sumukh Mehta from Bangalore is an inspiring one. He created a twenty-page magazine-style resume to apply for a marketing internship at GQ's London headquarters. Sumukh created a standout cover page and filled the inner pages with his skills, experiences and why he wanted to work at GQ. His personality radiated on every page. His resume rose to the top and caught the eye of Dylan Jones, editor-in-chief, British GQ. That got him both an interview and the internship.

It helps you stay relevant. Your personal brand is the way you can manage your relevance in the competitive world. David Beckham is a good example of someone who elevated his identity from a footballer to the multifaceted global icon that he is today. And he did this by constantly evolving his personal brand. No doubt establishing himself as a talented footballer was the starting point, but after that Beckham got involved in several things, all of which have helped him evolve and stay relevant long after the end of his footballing career. Some examples include collaborations with high-end fashion brands to add to his sense of style, involvement with philanthropic organisations like UNICEF, deep diving into the media world and appearing in films and reality shows, adventures in entrepreneurship (he invested in a football team and started a line of fragrance), being a cultural ambassador for the UK and also staying active and connected to the football world by launching his own MLS team and supporting the sport in emerging markets. He also uses social media expertly to showcase all these activities and his role as the ultimate family man. All these strategically thought-through initiatives have made him a global icon. Priyanka Chopra is another example of someone who transcended her initial industry (Bollywood) to achieve global recognition, relevance and influence. Her move to Hollywood sealed her image as a talented and versatile actor with broad appeal to international audiences. She ventured into the music industry and released a few chart-topping singles. She launched her own hair care brand, Anomaly. She is involved with UNICEF and other philanthropic ventures. Her production company, Purple Pebble Pictures, produces diverse and meaningful content that resonates with different audiences.

It helps you create an emotional connection. One aspect of having a personal brand is having something recognisable or unique to your personality. Canadian prime minister Justin

Trudeau is known for his colourful and quirky taste in socks. This creates an emotional connection with the public as it shows a bit of his personality away from the officialdom and formality that usually characterises public figures. His choice of socks can be a conversation starter, breaking down barriers between him and the people he serves. The socks also get talked about a lot on social media. All these elements contribute to him being viewed as an approachable and likeable personality, which become key characteristics of the Justin Trudeau brand notwithstanding recent India-Canada relations.

It helps you command a premium. Many celebrities have successfully leveraged their personal brands to command premium rates for their products, services or endorsements.

Oprah Winfrey is a great example. She has gone from TV host to a media queen by building a strong and trusted brand that the American public can relate to. She launched The Oprah Book Club and has created such a strong seal of endorsement that any book chosen by her for the book club becomes an instant bookseller. A lot of this has to do with her own credibility related to endorsing books and other products. However, celebrities are not alone in being able to command a premium from their personal brands.

The concept applies to many different professions such as:

CEOs and business leaders: The positive impact of their brands shows up in the share price of their companies. They can also command a greater premium for their company's products and services. Apple, Tesla and Coco Chanel are great examples.

Authors and thought leaders: The ones with stronger personal brands command more premium when it comes to publishing contracts, speaker engagements and other consulting assignments.

Consultants and coaches: If you have established a successful track record, you can charge more.

Influencers: Social media stars have the negotiating power for endorsements given their personal brands.

Health and wellness professionals: The stronger your personal brand through the content you produce, the certifications you have and your track record, the more sought after you will be in your industry.

Artists and other creatives: Those whose work is recognised as having a distinct style and identity, develop a strong reputation and can command a premium compared to the average artist.

Tech and industry experts: Those who are known for their deep expertise will be able to charge more for their advice or advisory role. They will also secure the highest paying jobs.

Educators and trainers: Even in the school tuition market, educators with strong personal brands are most sought after.

Legal and financial professionals: Lawyers and accountants with the strongest reputations are undeniably at the top of the league when it comes to fees.

Local experts and specialists: This assorted category can vary from chefs to wedding planners. Build a niche, develop your reputation, invest in your personal brand and you will reap the rewards.

So it's not just celebrities but also individuals in every professional category that have the potential to monetise their personal brands by commanding a premium in the market they serve.

A personal brand brings focus and clarity. When you know what you want to stand for, it allows you to make career choices accordingly. It gives you focus as well as clarity when faced with a multitude of choices.

Vidya Balan is very particular about the kind of roles she takes up in Bollywood which has cemented her reputation as an actress who takes on challenging roles.

Personal branding also galvanises people. Having a strong personal brand is helpful in influencing others and galvanising them to action.

Celebrity businesspeople like Ratan Tata, Sanjiv Mehta, Richard Branson, Kiran Mazumdar-Shaw and Indra Nooyi are some well-known figures who can positively impact thousands of lives through their messages.

All of these advantages of a personal brand will give you an idea of why it's so valuable.

The truth is, whether you like it or not, your personal brand is being built every day, by default, through your expressions and actions. Ask yourself if you want to control the narrative about you or want to be controlled by it. Would you rather your brand be built by default? Or would it benefit you to build it by design?

There are many risks of leaving it to chance. You won't be in charge of driving perceptions about brand YOU, others will be. How you want to project yourself may not be aligned with how others perceive you. The real value you bring to the world may not be clearly understood because you have not articulated it and communicated it to the world. You may be passed up for opportunities that you have been very keen on. In short, you may bleed into oblivion and the sea of sameness and not be remembered or recalled in the moments that matter.

On the other hand, as we have seen, the rewards to building your brand by yourself are manyfold. You can shape your destiny by clearly controlling the story you are telling the world about brand YOU because you are managing the message. There is a higher chance of others seeing you the way you want them to because you have been intentional about it by applying the tools of personal branding. Most importantly, you can drive faster towards your ambitions because you have a higher chance of being remembered in the moments that matter the most.

If this is personal branding, are you in?

Let's dive into the 5Ds of building a personal brand.

4

Act 1: Discover

'Knowing yourself is the beginning of all wisdom,' Aristotle famously said.

To build a strong personal brand, it is important to know yourself well. If you project yourself in a way that is not true to who you are, it risks coming across as inauthentic. Self-discovery will help you land on attributes that you are likely to sustain over a long period of time thus ensuring consistency, which is an important element of branding.

This quote by Aristotle reminds us that personal branding is not only about an image to be projected but also about an understanding of who you are and what is special about you, and then projecting this to the world. How you portray yourself should be an extension of your true self, not a depiction of how you want others to see you.

By making discovery the first step of the process, you can ensure that you will build a personal brand that is rooted in self-awareness and authenticity.

What do I mean by discovering yourself? You will have to spend time in deep self-exploration to zero in on your identity, values, beliefs, strengths, weaknesses, blind spots, passions and so on. It requires healthy doses of self-reflection and introspection.

What are some ways in which you can 'go in' to understand more about what is uniquely you?

There are many methods and frameworks for self-reflection. Some are discussed below.

General methods include journaling and meditation. If you set aside a regular time to reflect on your day and journal about it, the chances of you understanding yourself and your patterns are much higher. Journaling is often cited as the most effective way in which professionals learn about themselves based on their actions. Meditation is also a good way of shutting out the noise of the world. It greatly helps you think clearly.

Online personality assessments might also give you a greater understanding of who you are. Popular tests include MBTI (Myers-Briggs Type Indicator), StrengthsFinder and Enneagram. MBTI is popular with companies. Your co-workers are likely to have taken these assessments at some point in their careers so you can discuss your MBTI type with teammates and others.

The specific method that I recommend in the discovery phase of personal branding is the 360 Degree Perception Audit. It is the process of gathering anonymous feedback from multiple sources – peers, seniors, juniors, family, friends and personal advisors – about your performance, behaviour and reputation.

You can either use a formal online tool like the one offered by sites like Survey Monkey, or you can simply send questions directly to those from whom you are seeking feedback. With the direct survey, you may not get truthful feedback, which is why it's better to use an online tool where anonymity can be coded in the design of the survey.

There are three simple questions to ask:

1. What do you think are my biggest strengths? Please list a few key words.
2. What holds me back from achieving my full potential? In other words, what are my blind spots?
3. Anything else you would like me to know that can help me discover what is truly special about me and the value I can deliver to others?

I would suggest sending these questions via email or an online survey link to at least twenty people. That way, you will get a broad range of responses and you can look for the patterns emerging about your true strengths.

Be mentally prepared for what you will get back. People may say things that you may not like. Don't be defensive.

Acknowledge each response with a sincere thank you. Keep an open mind as you filter through all the comments.

You must also do a self-audit of how you perceive yourself. You can answer the same set of questions that you asked of others. You can also think about your passions and interests. One good way to know what you are good at or known for is to think about what most people come to you for.

Once you have enough data on how you are perceived by yourself and others, it's time to analyse the output using a framework that you may have studied in your high school or college psychology course. It's called the Johari Window. Think of it as a window with four panes.

The Johari Window was developed by psychologists Joseph Luft and Harry Ingham in 1955. It is named after a combination of their first names, Jo (Joseph) and Harry. This model was created as a tool to help individuals and groups improve their understanding of themselves and their relationships with others by visualising self-awareness and mutual awareness. The framework is taught in business schools as well to help prepare young managers for the workplace.

The Johari Window is a psychological model that represents a person's self-awareness and understanding of their relationship with others. It consists of four quadrants: open, blind, hidden and unknown.

	Known to self	**Not known to self**
Known to others	Open	Blind
Not known to others	Hidden	Unknown

These quadrants illustrate different aspects of information about an individual including what is 'known' and 'unknown' to themselves and others. The goal is to expand the 'open' quadrant by increasing self-disclosure and mutual understanding, ultimately enhancing communication and relationships.

So how can we apply the Johari Window to personal branding?

I love it as a discovery tool because it gives us clear direction on what to reveal about ourselves and what to make the anchor of our personal brand.

So how can you use this framework? Sift through all the feedback data you have from your 360 Degree Perception Audit. Put each data point in one of the four Johari Windows:

The first quadrant for things known to others and known to self: the Open area.

- What do you know about yourself that others know as well?
- Go back to your data collection and insert here the things that people said about you that you already know.

The second quadrant for that which is known to others but not known to self: the Blind area.

- What don't you know about yourself but others know about you?
- Qualities that other people see in us that we don't see in ourselves.
- Go back to your data collection and put in here the things that people said about you that were a surprise to you.

The third quadrant for what is not known to others but known to self: the Hidden area.

- What do you know about yourself that others don't know about you?
- What aspect of yourself might you be holding back from sharing with others?
- Go back to your data collection and put in here things about yourself that others may not perceive but you know is an asset.

The fourth quadrant for things not known to others and not known to self: the Unknown area.

- What do you not know about yourself and others don't know either?

- Go back to your data collection and look for evidence of your strengths, character, personality and likes and dislikes.
- If any of these categories are not reflected in the data, put it down in the unknown as it will help you take action to discover more about yourself.

If most of the data points are falling in 'unknown' then you need to work on self-development first before you try to establish a personal brand. This means that you are operating in a way that neither you nor others know what drives you, what defines you and what your inherent strengths are. I would suggest getting a personal coach or mentor to help you on this journey. Personal growth and self-discovery can help expand this quadrant over time. Without doing self-work, building a personal brand will be futile.

The Hidden area offers food for thought. Which of these gems do you want to reveal to the world and which ones do you want to keep hidden? Attributes about you that are currently hidden from the world could be brought out either in the master narrative about you or some sub-themes and messages.

The Blind area is important because you must know how people perceive you in a way that you don't perceive yourself. These attributes will need to be managed to establish your personal brand. For example, if you're positioning yourself as the most helpful doctor and your blind spot is lack of respect for others, then it will be difficult to deliver what you stand for. It would be important to address the feedback before you build your brand. You should not stand for something that is in direct contradiction to a blind spot you have.

The Open area is where the magic lies for defining your personal brand. Carefully think through all the data points here and how you might be able to weave a story about yourself that builds on these strengths, values, qualities and beliefs. This is fertile ground for defining and expanding your personal brand. Your close circle already believes this about you. Hence it can become the foundation for how you want to present yourself to the world.

Lulu's Johari Window

	Known to self	**Not known to self**
Known to others	Open • Warm • Energetic • Passionate • Owns the room • Influential • Positive drive	Blind • Discipline • Humble • Kind
Not known to others	Hidden • Love to help others • Ambition to be an influential global leader	Unknown • Things about me that upset others

Let me walk you through how using this framework helped me define my personal brand better.

When I did the survey to ask my friends, family and co-workers about their perceptions of me, I got a long list of attributes to work with.

It was easy to slot attributes in the Open area. I know that I am warm, energetic, passionate, influential, driven and can own the room. These are things I needed to amplify in my personal brand.

What was most interesting to me were the things about myself that I didn't recognise as things that stood out to others – the attributes in the Blind area. I learned that people see me as disciplined, humble and kind.

What I also learned was that I was not necessarily showcasing my ambition to be a global leader. Additionally, my love for helping others wasn't coming through as powerfully. These I slotted in the Hidden area.

Through this process I realised I didn't fully grasp the things about me that upset others. All my feedback was positive and that couldn't be entirely true. I needed to learn more and hence that unknown was an area for more self-discovery.

When you read Act 2 on definition, you'll see how this comes together for me. The summary is that I have fused a few attributes from my Blind area (humble, kind) with a few strengths in the Open area (Influential, positive drive) to define the personality of my personal brand as a 'gentle force.' I couldn't have arrived at this without the Johari Window exercise.

To summarise, the Johari Window tool helps you see how others see you, it improves your self-awareness and is a good starting point to define your personal brand.

We will discuss more about defining your personal brand in the next chapter.

5

Act 2: Define

ONCE YOU HAVE COLLECTED the data on perceptions about Brand YOU, it's time to define your personal brand.

The most important question to answer when defining your personal brand is this: what do I want to stand for that creates value for others?

In the professional world of marketing and brand building, there are many ways frameworks are used to define a brand. A very popular one is the Brand Key model, which is used by Unilever to define its product brands. Another is the Brand Identity Prism developed by Jean-Noel Kapferer. At Landor, we use the Brand Driver Platform.

After studying all these models, I've culled three elements that are useful in the context of defining your personal brand: purpose, positioning and personality. Defining these three aspects of your personal brand serves as foundational work in creating a successful and memorable brand strategy that drives the creation of your brand identity.

Many people make the mistake of starting to communicate on social media thinking they are launching and building their brand. Often, however, they skip the important pre-work of defining their brand. This is where brand strategy comes in.

Strategy must always precede the tactics. Otherwise, you will miss out on establishing a clear direction, ensuring differentiation and maintaining consistency. Clarity on what you want to stand for will guide decision-making when creating posts for social media. It will also help to build an emotional connection with your audience because you would have done the work on thinking through how you are relevant for them.

Purpose

Purpose is a succinct and motivating reason to exist. Why do you do what you do? What motivates and energises you? Why do you wake up every morning full of energy for the day ahead?

Here's an example of a purpose statement I developed for my personal brand: 'Lulu Raghavan is a brand evangelist who is passionate about using the power of branding and design to create commercial impact for companies, social impact for brands and non-profits and personal legacy for individuals.'

It may be useful to use the five-whys technique here. It is a design thinking technique used to get to the heart or root cause of something and not just settle with the surface level response.

Ask yourself five whys. Here are some of mine:
Why do you wake up every morning?
I wake up because I am excited about helping renowned brands who have lost their path rise to prominence again.

Why is that important to you?
I like working on big brands.

Why is that important?
Getting a big brand back on track would give me a sense of accomplishment of creating impact on a large scale.

Why is that important to you?
Because I want to use my talent to make a difference.

Why is that important?
I believe in living life to my full potential.

You can see how the five-whys technique can highlight your underlying motivations and drivers.

There are many benefits of having a clear purpose. It articulates your vision and acts as your North Star. Your purpose can motivate, energise and galvanise others as you connect with them at an emotional level.

The cost of not having a purpose means that you may lack motivation on some days. You may function like a rudderless ship. When you don't have that conviction and clarity, it will be harder to emotionally connect with others.

Things to reflect on:
What are your core values and beliefs? What motivates you to do what you do? What are you passionate about that can make a difference to the world? What are your unique strengths and talents that you can use to achieve your goals. Who are you creating value for? What can you give them that they will deeply care about?

Try this:
Write your obituary. Write it in 140 words or less.

Imagine someone is tweeting about you just after learning about your passing. Think about the value you created in the world, who you created it for and the impact it had on them.

While this may sound like a morbid exercise, it is a very popular exercise in my personal branding workshops. Every time I have shared this with audiences, the feedback has ranged from eye-opening to transformational. When you start to think about your own mortality, you not only realise that you have very little time on this earth but also that you should be less selfish and strive to create more impact before it is too late.

For inspiration, read the *New York Times* obituaries. It gives you a sense of the kind of impact people make in the world that is valued by others.

In *Show Your Work*, author Austin Kleon has this to say about obituaries:

'Obituaries aren't really about death; they are about life. "The sum of every obituary is how heroic people are, and how noble," writes Maira Kalman. Reading about people who are dead now and did things with their lives makes me want to get up and do something decent with mine. Thinking about death every morning makes me want to live.'

Positioning

While purpose is about you alone, positioning is a competitive frame. As part of defining your personal brand, you have to think through what is your unique strength versus others'. Are you the first in a field? Are you the only one? Are you better? In what way are you better?

Positioning helps you think through how you are relevant to those you want to serve in a way that is different from others who are serving the same people.

Take the world of Bollywood actors. There are the three famous Khans – Aamir Khan, Shah Rukh Khan and Salman Khan. A Khan is a Khan, right? Actually, each one has positioned himself quite uniquely. Aamir is the 'intellectual' Khan, Shah Rukh is the 'romantic' Khan and Salman is the 'man of the masses' Khan. They share the same last name but have distinct positioning.

What is the thing that only you do very well? Martin Neumeier, author of dozens of books on branding, calls this your 'onlyness'? What is your onlyness?

The benefits of having a clear positioning are numerous. It distils who you are. It articulates your point of differentiation. It makes it easier to connect with your audience. The biggest cost of not having a clear positioning is getting lost in the sea of sameness and not standing out.

Questions to reflect on:
Ask yourself what specific area or expertise you want to focus on. Who is your target audience? What are their needs and pain points that you can serve? What unique value do you bring to the table and how does it solve your target audience's problems? What sets you apart from others in your field? What makes you unique or different? How do you want to be perceived by your target audience and what kind of reputation do you want to build?

Try this:
Write your elevator pitch.

You are in a job interview when you are asked to tell the interviewer about yourself. What is the crispest and most succinct version of your answer? Can you respond in ten words or less?

List down your skills, your credibility, your strengths and your values. Think about all the data points in your Open area from the Johari Window exercise. Are there attributes in your Hidden area or Blind area, waiting to be brought forward to define your positioning?

Here's a freelance writer's positioning statement before the exercise:

I am a freelance writer specialising in long-form content for B2B technology companies. I help my clients communicate complex ideas in a clear and engaging way, positioning them as thought leaders in their industry. With over 10 years of experience in the tech sector, I bring a deep understanding of my clients' needs and a unique perspective to every project I take on.

Here's their positioning statement after the exercise:

I help my clients communicate complex ideas very clearly.

Which one is easier to understand? Which one is more memorable? Which one has a greater impact? Hopefully you can see the world of difference between the two. Shorter and simpler is always more effective.

It won't be easy to nail your elevator pitch. Use all the input you have gathered in the discovery phase to help you craft and hone your pitch to be as sharp as possible.

In case you struggle with cracking your elevator pitch, you can try writing a longer positioning statement first.

Use this format:

In a world characterised by __________ (some pain point related to your profession)

I am the only ___________ (definition of how you see yourself)

Who ____________ (key value you bring to the table)

Because I ___________ (the benefit you deliver).

Here's an example of a positioning statement I developed for myself:

In a world characterised by brand consultants who sound and look alike

I am the only brand consultant who is also an evangelist

Passionately and tirelessly advocating for the benefits of branding and design beyond surface level

And showing companies, non-profits and individuals how brands can help them create an impact.

Personality

When thinking through the definition of your personal brand, you will have the most fun with the personality part. This is how you can truly play up your differentiation. It is also how you ensure a consistent tone of voice that reflects how you want to be perceived.

Think of the different airline brands in India. Air India, SpiceJet, Go First Air or Indigo. Which one truly has a personality? Indigo, right? From the way their staff interacts with you to their witty ads and the language they use across different touch points, their quirky personality shines through. This is not to say that being witty and funny is the only way to have a distinct personality.

Vistara is more polite and formal. Air India is more Indian for sure. Indigo is witty and fun.

How do you want to project yourself? When brands do this, they may choose a battery of words that define them. Dove, the beauty brand from Unilever projects innocence, authenticity and honesty. Virgin is a maverick, rebellious, sexy brand.

Try this:
What is your two-word brand personality?

Sometimes it's good to choose just two words about yourself which have some inherent tension between the two.

I have defined the personality of my personal brand as a 'gentle force'.

When someone is referred to as a 'gentle force', it typically means that they possess a quiet strength or influence. They have the ability to make a positive impact on others or effect change in a subtle and compassionate manner. I want others to see me as both gentle and powerful, combining a sense of kindness and empathy with an underlying strength and determination.

What is your visual brand driver?

Another useful tool is to build for yourself what we at Landor call a visual brand driver. Create a big square box with 9 smaller boxes (3x3). Each box represents one category.

Here's an example for how to use a visual brand driver. Find a picture that best represents your personality in each of these categories:

MAGAZINE	FAMOUS PERSON	VEHICLE
WATCH	FURNITURE	DRINK
ACTIVITY	ANIMAL	CITY

1. If you were a magazine, what magazine personifies you?
2. If you were a famous person, which famous person personifies you?
3. If you were a vehicle, what vehicle personifies you?
4. If you were a watch, what watch personifies you?
5. If you were a piece of furniture, what furniture personifies you?
6. If you were a drink, what drink personifies you?
7. If you were an activity, what activity personifies you?
8. If you were an animal, what animal personifies you?
9. If you were a city, which city personifies you?

When you start to think about whether you are more of a dolphin or a whale, more like Mumbai or more like Tokyo, you start to see patterns about who you are and how you want to be perceived. In the workshops I've conducted, participants love this part of defining their brand strategy the most.

The way in which this exercise is useful is that it brings out your personality clearly. If you chose the dolphin as the animal in the above exercise for example, you see yourself as open, friendly and agile. The city you choose indicates the energy and vibe that represents your spirit. For example, you may be more high-octane (New York) than chilled out (Goa). This projective technique of choosing images allows you to surface aspects of your personality which you may not articulate when just asked to list words.

When you work through the combination of purpose, positioning and personality, you have defined your brand strategy. You have clarity on why you do what you do, the value you bring to the table for others and the way in which you deliver your message and do your work. You are now ready for the next step which is to design the different elements of your personal brand.

6

Act 3: Design

DO YOU WISH YOU had what it takes to light up the room when you arrive? How do you create a powerful impact even before you have said something? How do you dress? What is the vibe exude? Are you projecting power and confidence, or do you look nervous and about to be overwhelmed by the moment?

What are the first impressions about you when someone visits your website or sees one of your posts on social media? Even the way you communicate on email can make a strong first impression or a poor one.

This is where the 'design' of your personal brand can make a big difference.

I like to think of the design of your personal brand as the elements that can create memorability and be recalled when someone hears your name.

There are three categories of assets you can create which will help you build your personal brand: visual assets, verbal assets and proxy assets.

Visual Assets

Choose a signature style. A coach who is popular in the advertising industry always wears long kurtas on jeans. It makes him more approachable to youngsters who are intimidated by the formality that surrounds their bosses. The coach uses this as a way to connect better with his target audience and to also stand out in a crowd in industry events.

Choose a colour or combination of colours. When my company's brand colour was primarily yellow, I used to make it a point to have something yellow on me for key client meetings.

I had quite a few pieces of clothing which were yellow. I also had a yellow laptop bag, a few pens, a notebook and some other tchotchkes. To this day, so many clients remark when I am not dressed in yellow. This is because they have strong associations of yellow with me in their mind. When Landor rebranded, we adopted an ultramarine blue with no yellow in the visual system. So many clients and friends lamented the loss of yellow!

Design a logo. Create a visual mnemonic you can use on your website and all your social media assets. I developed a distinct 'LR' logo in yellow and black which communicates both strength and humility – my personality attributes. You can see my logo on the back cover of this book.

Choose a font. If you create a lot of posts with text, a distinct and consistent typeface can help you stand out.

Curate your professional photos. It's a good idea to invest in some stock photos of yourself taken by a highly qualified professional photographer that you can upload as your profile, especially on LinkedIn. In the age of mobile phone cameras, it is tempting to save money here, but the results won't be as professional as you desire. LinkedIn profiles with highly professional photos stand out. If the photo communicates your personality clearly, all the more effective.

Jyotika Purwar, Founder and Creative Director, Walter & the Studio, on Creative Tips

Designing your personal brand is an exciting journey that should reflect the essence of who you are. Here are some tips to kickstart your visual identity creative process:

1. Calendar some creative zen time: Set aside dedicated moments in your week for this creative endeavour. Clear away distractions, like social media pings, and treat it like a zen meditation session for your imagination.
2. Moodboard magic: Collect inspiration throughout the week, be it snapshots of joy inducing images or digital ideas on Pinterest. Curate images that resonate with you and that spark your creativity.
3. Words that represent your brand: Jot down a list of words that define 'you'. Do you want your brand to burst with energy, exude calmness, embody elegance or tickle with humour? Let your personality traits guide your choices.

4. Discover your colour: Selecting a colour for your brand isn't just about favourites. It's about vibes! Warm hues for energetic souls, cool tones for those who exude calm or neutrals for the minimalists. Take the fun personality quiz 'The Color of My Personality' for a colourful self-discovery.
5. Which font are you: Fonts speak volumes about your brand's personality. Serif, sans-serif or signature, each has its own language. Use Google Fonts for a wide selection that won't break the bank. Consistent font usage not only reinforces your brand identity but also ensures recognition, particularly on social media posts.
6. Symbol (to include or exclude): Adding a distinctive and unique symbol to your visual identity can help shape how you're perceived in a glance and can become a strong and effective part of your brand. It is your personal choice to decide if your brand is best represented by a symbol, a wordmark or your signature.
7. Experiment Freely: When crafting your brand, consider its versatility across platforms. Ask yourself, does your visual identity lend itself to multimedia dimensions like music, animation and video?
8. DIY or Pro Power: Craft your brand assets using DIY tools like Canva for hands-on creativity. For a more polished touch, platforms like 99 Designs provide a professional edge. And of course, there's always the option to enlist the expertise of a seasoned pro (like me!).
9. Create, Tweak, Repeat: Building your personal brand isn't a one-time sprint but an ongoing process of creativity. Tweak, refine and evolve as you grow.

Your brand is a dynamic entity that should resonate through every chapter of your professional journey. These tips are a compass, guiding you through the creation of a personal brand. Let the world see the masterpiece that is uniquely you!

Verbal Assets

You can also stand out with others based on the words you use. In an earlier example I talked about how author Todd Henry says he is 'an arm's dealer for creative professionals.'

Here are some more examples of what professionals might use as a tagline.

'Elevating Brands with Digital Magic': A digital marketing specialist or social media strategist known for their creative and effective digital campaigns.

'Cultivating Leaders, Cultivating Success': A leadership development coach or trainer.

'Building Sustainable Futures': An environmental activist, architect or consultant focusing on sustainable design and practices.

'Navigating Complex Legal Waters': A lawyer or legal consultant specialising in complex legal matters.

Taglines should not be just empty words or promises. They have to be delivered by these professionals in every interaction they have with their audiences.

Beyond taglines, you should also channel a particular brand voice (sometimes known as tone of voice) in your communications – emails, blogs, posts, etc. For this, you have to choose a particular style and translate that into principles and guidelines.

Let's take my own example of 'a gentle force' and see how that translates to my brand voice.

Here are the things that I keep in mind when communicating (while speaking or writing), which are consistent with my personal brand of being a gentle force.

Empathy and understanding

I like to show genuine empathy and understanding in my messaging. I address the needs, concerns and feelings of my audience with compassion. I try to be less self-centred and keep the audience at the front and centre. For example, if I'm asking for help, I usually give the person an easy way to say no to create no pressure.

Clarity and confidence

I like to communicate with clarity and confidence. I clearly articulate my message and purpose while exuding supreme confidence in my abilities to make a positive impact.

Inclusivity

I embrace inclusivity and diversity in my language and imagery. For example, I used to say 'Hi guys' to address the team but now I say 'Hi everyone'. A simple change but an important one in an era of gender fluidity. I try to make all individuals feel valued and included. This is especially important in team meetings where a few people can end up dominating the space if you are not careful. Part of my style is to ask for the opinions of those who are shy to contribute or speak up in a meeting.

Positive reinforcement

I love to use positive language and messaging to uplift and inspire. I try to highlight the positive outcomes in any situation. I am a huge believer in the power of transformative vocabulary. When you focus on the positive, it amplifies. This is especially true when motivating teammates.

Listening and feedback

I encourage feedback and active listening. I like to show that I am receptive to input and committed to continuous improvement.

Support and guidance

I position myself as a supportive guide and mentor. I offer valuable insights, advice and resources to help others overcome challenges. I often get requests on social media for mentoring, which means that my brand voice is clearly communicating this aspect.

Respect and politeness

I maintain a very polite and respectful tone in all my interactions. I have found that treating others with courtesy and consideration not only uplifts my own mood but pays off hugely in the long run. So few people pay attention to this that you can really stand out by making this a signature component of your style.

Balanced strength

I try to strike a balance of strength with gentleness. I try to show how my power and influence has been used with compassion and kindness to achieve positive results. By channelling these principles, I demonstrate a distinct brand voice consistent with my personal brand definition in all my communications. This then serves as a powerful tool in my verbal assets' arsenal.

Proxy Assets

How do you use others to say things about you that are consistent with your personal brand? This is an equally important, if not more important, aspect of personal brand design. It is designing or subtly influencing what others say about you.

Word of mouth is the most popular and effective means to market yourself. You don't have to over-engineer this one. By being your authentic self-day in and day out, you will automatically create positive word of mouth. The things people say about you will be directly taken from the key messages that you are putting out about yourself. If your messages are consistent with your personal brand definition, this will be easily accomplished.

Another such asset is to have recommendations from a select set of people. While I haven't used this feature on LinkedIn or on my website, this is a good one for those who may be shy of speaking about their achievements and uniqueness. Here you can ask a few highly credible professionals to endorse you publicly. It would be good to explain your personal brand to them so that whatever they write will match-up. Don't make the mistake of writing the recommendation for them or being too prescriptive. It will stink of inauthenticity and therefore defeat the purpose.

You may also intentionally want to recruit your band of personal evangelists who will speak up about you when it matters. These could be highly influential professionals in the corporate world or in your community. Here again, by taking them through your personal brand, you are increasing the chances of them talking about you in the way you want others to see you.

Komal Ramani-Makhija, personal brand expert on developing unique visual and verbal assets

How many people do you meet in a day? Or see online in a day? How many of them stick in your memory?

This is where design consistency comes to the rescue! It can help you stand out and be heard in a room full of loudspeakers. It's like crafting your brand's DNA – giving it a specific character and direction.

You can achieve this by using a unique color, an illustration, a caricature, a signature writing style or a combination of these elements. But it is when you show up consistently – with the same avatar across all channels like social media, promotions and email signatures – that people start to remember you, associate with you and create a mental image of you. The clearer the image, the greater the impact of your personal brand.

Take Oprah Winfrey or Michelle Obama, for instance. We see them on various occasions and platforms, yet every time we hear them, our perception of their persona becomes clearer. This effect is the result of consistency. It is the result of using conscious colour, tone, words, again and again, when you speak to your audience, irrespective of the platform you are on.

7

Act 4: Deploy

Once you've spent time discovering, defining and designing your brand, it's time to bring it all together in the form of your personal brand guidelines and think about the modes of deployment.

Personal brand guidelines is a key tool to ensure there is alignment between your personal brand strategy and its execution. You've been intentional about how you want to be perceived. Now you must be equally intentional about how you show up at every touch point that makes an impression on others.

'Strategy on a page' is becoming more common in the corporate world. It is a concise and visual representation of a business strategy that can be quickly communicated and understood. The 'strategy on a page' provides a clear and concise overview of the organisation's vision, mission, values, strategic focus areas, objectives, initiatives, KPIs, budget allocation and risk analysis. It serves as a reference point for the entire organisation, aligning efforts toward common goals and ensuring everyone understands the overarching strategy.

Similarly, you would benefit from 'Brand YOU on a page' to provide a clear roadmap for building and maintaining your personal brand.

Brand YOU on a Page

DISCOVER

Use the attributes from your 360 Brand Perception Audit to fill out your Johari Window.

The Johari Window

	Known to Self	**Not Known to Self**
Known to Others	Open Area	Blind Spot
Not Known to Others	Hidden Area	Unknown

DEFINE

PURPOSE

Write your obituary

The value you created in the world +
Who you had created it for + Impact it had
Use 140 words or less

POSITIONING

Positioning statement

In a world characterised by _________ (some pain point related to your profession)
I am the only __________ (definition of how you see yourself)
Who ___________ (key value you bring to the table)
Because I __________ (the benefit you deliver).

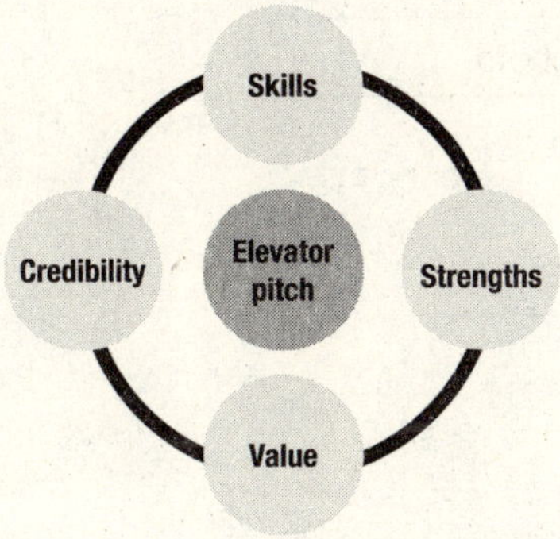

PERSONALITY

Visual Brand Driver

Describe an image or two for each category that best describes your personality.

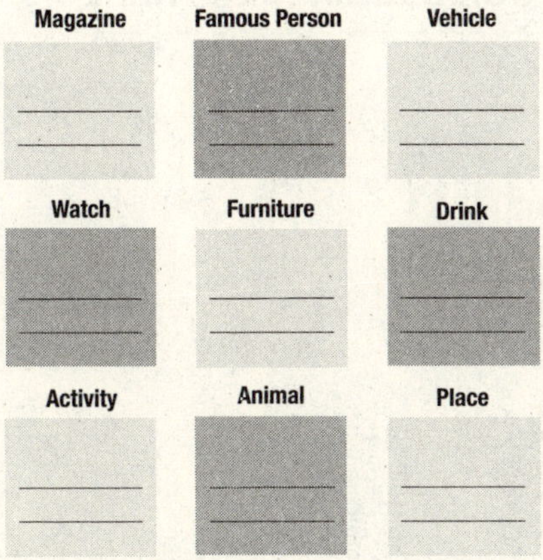

DESIGN

Visual assets

Logo

Typeface

Colours

Professional photo

Verbal assets

Tagline

Brand voice

Proxy assets

Word of mouth

Formal recommendations

Personal evangelists

JOT DOWN YOUR DESIGN IDEAS HERE

SCRATCH PAD FOR YOUR NOTES

You can use this easy framework to ensure all the elements you have previously worked on are easily accessible to you.

It might be helpful to think of 'on-brand' and 'off-brand' as you go about deploying your brand.

On-brand is when you consistently represent yourself in a way that reinforces how you wish to be perceived which includes maintaining a positive professional image, sharing content that aligns with your personal brand and consistently showing up.

Off-brand is when you show up in a way that is not consistent with how you wish to be perceived. If you see yourself as calm but lose your cool often, that is off-brand. If you see yourself as witty but your social media is bland and boring, that is off-brand. Expressions and actions that are not in line with BrandYOU are considered off-brand.

The way to build personal brand equity is through consistently deploying on-brand tactics – your expressions and actions need to reflect BrandYOU.

Let us now look at some high impact ways in which you can deploy your personal brand.

Your Personal Website

Your personal website hands down is the most effective tool you have at your disposal today to influence perceptions of who you are.

Ideally, you should secure firstnamelastname.com. For example, my website is: http://luluraghavan.com.

Your website is your golden opportunity to curate your image and present yourself to the world just the way you want it. Everything from the design to the words are chosen by you. You are in full control of showing the world the best version of yourself.

As I've said before, thought must come before design. Before you start designing your website or hiring a professional web designer to help you, think about the strategy.

The easiest way is to make your personal brand website your glorified curriculum vitae. This is the way to go if you're looking to get hired. It's a much fuller and more dynamic representation of your candidature for recruiters than a one-page resume. Your personality can shine through, and it can, in a few seconds, give people a good sense of who you are and what you believe in. Many years ago, I was guiding Pallavi, a young graduate in the US, and I gave her the suggestion of building her website to enhance her resume and to stand out with recruiters. She took my guidance to heart and created an impactful personal website showcasing her skills and expertise, which helped her land a job more easily.

You've already defined your purpose, positioning and personality. You have all your branding elements. Now think about the audience for your website. Who do you want to reach with your message and what might be some of their pain points your personal brand can address? What do you want to accomplish with your website? Do you want to attract new opportunities? Do you want to get more followers? Do you want a better platform to showcase your work?

Once you've set your goals, you can determine what content you want to have on your website – blog posts, photos, videos, portfolio, etc. – and the frequency at which you will publish fresh content.

Outline the navigation and structure of your website. This is called website architecture which shows the flow between pages for a someone who lands on your website.

Consider all your branding elements defined earlier and the UX as well. UX is user experience and includes elements to think through such as time to load a website, easy-to-find information, call to action, etc.

You may choose to invest in search engine optimisation (SEO) by identifying key words relevant to your personal brand and including them on your website.

You may also want to consider how to integrate your social media handles into your website design. This is a great way to drive traffic between different media channels.

All the above are not comprehensive steps but a few key things you will want to consider when embarking on developing your personal brand website.

Social Media

You don't have to be active on social media to build your personal brand, but you must be conscious of two things.

The first thing is that if you are on social media but not conscious about the content you are posting and what it reflects about you, you may accidentally create wrong impressions of who you are. People are watching all the time and whether you like it or not your brand is being built. So if you are on social media, you have to have an intentional strategy.

The second thing is if you choose to plunge in intentionally, you must be consistent. Don't start if you don't have the time and energy to dedicate to it. You don't have to post content at high frequency (every day) but at least once a week (depending on the channel) is a must to keep your audience engaged and to grow your network.

So how do you choose the social media channels?

The most popular ones for professional brand building include LinkedIn, X (formerly Twitter), Instagram and YouTube.

It's important to have a strategic intent for each channel. Don't fall into the trap of cutting and pasting the same posts on each channel.

LinkedIn is a must. It is an absolute necessity to build your personal brand because it focuses on professional networking, offers tools for showcasing expertise and provides numerous opportunities for engagement and visibility within your industry and beyond. By actively managing and optimising your LinkedIn presence, you can strengthen your personal brand and unlock a host of professional opportunities.

X is better for those who have more time to dedicate as it requires consistent effort. People who enjoy words more than images tend to prefer X. It's also a great way to tune in to conversations happening in different industries and sub-groups.

Instagram is great for those who have a lot of visual content or those who don't mind sharing photos from their work and personal lives. It's a way of developing a more intimate connection with your audience as it tends to be less formal than LinkedIn. For example, I may post a photo of my family on Instagram, something I would never do on LinkedIn.

YouTube is the most time intensive as it requires a lot of thought, time and energy to produce. While you don't have to only produce videos of high production quality, these videos can expose a lot more of you so you must be cautious about what you post.

There's plenty of guidance on each of these channels which you can find online, and I would suggest a deep dive into each before choosing them. Your choice may also be guided by your profession and where your community gathers more frequently for conversations and inspiration. Writers seem to congregate on X, visual artists on Instagram and businesspeople on LinkedIn.

My brand strategy entails primarily LinkedIn and Instagram. On LinkedIn, I showcase thought leadership and am also an ambassador for my company. I've chosen brand, design and leadership as key topics to talk about. I try to be as helpful to my audience as possible. It is less about trumpeting my own achievements and more about knowledge sharing.

On Instagram, which is more visually driven, I like to showcase where I am in the world as I feel the platform lends itself to sharing gorgeous photos of my travels. It's a nice way to build a rapport with my followers, especially using the Instagram Stories feature, where people respond more frequently than on the comments section of posts. I showcase our branding work for different clients. I do many talks and so I share the links. I also like to share book recommendations with my followers – this tends to be very popular. Inspired by a colleague, I have also started collating all my book recommendations in the Highlights section of my profile on Instagram.

I have been consistent with these two platforms for over a decade. I can tell you confidently and without any doubt that a consistent presence and sharing of high quality and relevant content on these two social media platforms have very strongly contributed to building my personal brand.

Some opportunities I have received from these two channels include an invitation to write a foreword for someone's book, a huge opportunity to lead a high-profile panel discussion on women in leadership at the ET Global Business Summit, an invitation to teach a course on personal branding at a well-known business school and multiple invitations to be on awards juries, to name just a few.

E-book

While publishing a book may be daunting, have you considered an e-book? E-books are rising in popularity and are fast becoming an effective way to demonstrate thought leadership, expertise and your point of view.

During the Covid-19 pandemic, Ronita Mukerjee, one of my colleagues, started collecting insights on changing consumer behaviour. I suggested to her that she collate her insights and publish it as an e-book. So, she curated twenty insights, wrote a short paragraph on each, added a relevant illustration and then strung the whole book together along with a foreword from me. She published it as a PDF on LinkedIn and surprised herself with the incredible traction she got. It reinforced her desire to be seen as a consumer-focused brand consultant. And the e-book became an important part of her portfolio.

What subjects are you passionate about? Is there a point of view on a topic that you are dying to share with the world? Consider publishing an e-book to build your personal brand and associate it strongly with a key area of expertise.

Ronita Mukerjee, Executive Client Director at Landor, on writing an e-book.

Do you remember the first lock down in 2020? So many of us took to baking. I tried and realised quickly I was better with words than cake batter. So, I started writing things I observed around me. We sent food packages to friends to fill the void created by 'social distancing'. Our living rooms became dynamic spaces for work and play.

I was fascinated with changing consumer behaviour. Encouraged by the positive comments on LinkedIn, I curated more than twenty 'Lockdown Musings' and their impact on brands. The icing on the proverbial cake was when Lulu suggested I turn my posts into an e-book. Nervous and excited, I decided to take the leap.

A year later, I self-published my first e-book. *Lockdown Musings* started as a passion project. And thanks to Lulu's thoughtful advice, it unlocked so many opportunities for me.

My personal brand as a thinker, writer and a passionate consumer expert was strengthened. I was more confident when I pitched new thinking ideas to clients. I realised the importance of 'passion projects' and how they can positively impact your energy. I was always brimming with ideas that influenced my work. It made me a better contributor.

I made many personal and professional connections who I now count as allies. I reached out to experts and writers I admired and sought their feedback on my book draft. I was pleasantly surprised with how generous everyone was with their time and support.

Above all, I identified my personal style of thought leadership. Simply put, I am a curious optimist.

Public Speaking

Another way to deploy your personal brand is to speak at public forums. If public speaking frightens you, find a way to overcome it as this is one of the fastest ways to build your personal brand.

You may not immediately get invited to speak at the most prestigious conferences. I certainly didn't. A good place to start is to go back to your undergrad or graduate school and start with guest lectures or mentoring sessions for students. This is a great way to practise in a relatively low stakes environment. The schools like to publicise these events on their social media platforms, which is helpful in building your personal brand.

Once you get better at public speaking, you should post links to your talks on your website and social media platforms. This is a good way of signalling your value to the world, which is a helpful start to building your personal brand.

Networking Events

To grow your network you must invest time in going to new forums and building your contacts by forging new relationships. Keith Ferrazzi's book *Never Eat Alone*, which I've written about in the previous section, is a wonderful read to gain more confidence in this area. Being strategic about attending events to grow your network is an important way to deploy your personal brand.

Google Search

When people ask me how I built such a strong personal brand, my two-word answer is: Google Search.

Google Search is a powerful tool for building and managing your personal brand in the digital age. It offers a platform to showcase your expertise, control your online narrative and connect with a global audience. By proactively managing your online presence and optimising it for search engines, you can strengthen your personal brand and seize various opportunities for personal and professional growth.

It's your First Moment of Truth (FMOT). How often have you 'Googled' someone you have to meet or someone whose name was mentioned? Don't you immediately get a sense of them after looking through news mentions, photos and videos of that person? It's often the first place people turn to when looking for information about individuals, products or services. Having a strong presence in Google search results ensures that you are visible to a wide audience.

It can enhance your credibility and trustworthiness. The endorsements you have – publications that carry articles you have written, forums you have spoken at, photo and videos of you in your professional avatar – establish your authority. This leads people to potentially trust you even before they have met you.

It gives you a competitive advantage. In many industries, having a strong and positive online presence is a competitive advantage. It can set you apart from others and make you the preferred choice for employers, clients or collaborators. This is especially true for consultants. In my field, which is brand consulting and design, standing out on Google Search has meant that clients who approach us already have a degree of confidence about the people and agency they are going to buy into.

It's a great way to showcase your content. Google Search allows you to showcase your expertise and accomplishments. If you have a personal website, a blog or social media profiles, they can rank in search results and serve as platforms to share your knowledge and experiences.

You don't have to rig Google Search and be obsessed with key words and rankings, but you should Google yourself every few months to monitor what's appearing about you. In cases where an appearance may not be favourable, try to get it taken down. In some cases, it may not be possible. Knowing what's out there and what others see will help you navigate potentially awkward conversations.

To summarise this section of deploying your personal brand: it's a great way to share content, build your authentic self, increase your visibility, establish your reputation, grow trust through consistency and deliver on your personal brand goals.

You don't have to choose all these methods of deployment (and there are many more) but choosing a few will surely give you a great advantage. You can then consistently cruise in fifth gear on your highway to accolades and achievements.

8

Act 5: Deliver

IF YOU'VE DONE ALL the work required of you in the first four acts, you are now ready to build equity in your personal brand with every opportunity you get, both online and offline.

The Three Cs

It's useful to remember the 3Cs of personal brand building to deliver your brand: clarity, consistency and credibility.

Clarity

Don't lose sight of how you have defined your personal brand whether that is through your purpose, positioning, personality, or tagline. Always keep this front and centre. It will help you make better choices with opportunities that come your way. It will also help others to understand you better when you are clear on the value you offer.

Suppose you are a marketing professional specialising in social media strategy. Your clarity could involve defining your niche and unique selling points, such as:

- Crafting a concise elevator pitch. For example, you could say, 'I help small businesses grow their online presence and increase engagement through tailored social media strategies.'
- Creating a professional website and LinkedIn profile that clearly states your services, skills and target audience.
- Using specific keywords related to social media marketing and small businesses in all your professional communications.

Consistency

Aim to show up in a consistent way as much as you can. You've defined your personality. So now stick within those boundaries. Consistency involves maintaining a uniform and cohesive image and message across all your interactions and touchpoints, whether online or offline. Use a consistent tone, style and messaging in your communication. It's about reinforcing your brand identity consistently. Behaving in a way inconsistent with your brand will hinder creating consistent impressions.

As the marketing professional specialising in social media strategy, you should be:

- Ensuring that your social media profiles (LinkedIn, Twitter, Instagram) all have the same profile picture, bio and branding elements.
- Regularly posting content that aligns with your expertise, such as tips on social media marketing, case studies and industry news, at consistent intervals (e.g., weekly blog posts, daily tweets).
- Delivering consistent quality in your work and interactions, such as providing high-quality service to clients and responding to messages professionally and promptly.

Credibility

This is the most important of the 3Cs. It's the thing that builds trust and attracts opportunities for you. It is also the most responsible for character-building. How do you build credibility? Deliver on your promises. Do what you are going to say you will. Keep your commitments. Don't be a flake. Respond to messages promptly. Return calls. Beyond this, you must, of course, invest in writing and speaking opportunities that enhance your credibility in your area of expertise.

Some additional ways in which you could build credibility as a social media specialist:

- Sharing testimonials and success stories from satisfied clients on your website and social media to showcase the effectiveness of your work.

- Publishing articles, whitepapers or eBooks on topics related to social media strategy, demonstrating your knowledge and thought leadership.
- Speaking at industry conferences, participating in webinars or being a guest on relevant podcasts to share your insights and experiences.
- Obtaining relevant certifications or continuing education in your field to reinforce your expertise and commitment to professional growth.

When you are clear about who you are and what you stand for, maintain consistency in your messaging and actions and build credibility through your expertise and reputation, you are more likely to succeed in establishing a strong and memorable personal brand.

Personal Board of Advisors

Recruiting an informal personal board of advisors is a game-changing idea that can help enhance the delivery of your brand. You benefit from the experience and expertise of a select few who can guide you on your journey with useful insights, connections, moral support and constant encouragement.

Think of these people as advisors and well-wishers that you meet from time to time, say a few times a year. You keep them updated on your progress and development while seeking feedback and fresh perspectives.

Who are these people? They could be family, friends, industry peers, clients or colleagues. They are people with whom you have developed some sort of special connection. You both feel invested in each other and want to help each other grow. Sometimes you may have more to give, sometimes it may be the other person. Don't be disheartened that you don't have much to offer – you always have something to give, even if it is your time, attention and patient listening.

Your personal board of advisors is meant to ensure you are always seeing things from a broader perspective and that you remain accountable for your goals. Some of your board members may introduce you to movers and shakers in their network, others may help you through tough times and a few may truly push you beyond your comfort zone. Some may add value by just being there for you.

I find it useful to tell someone I'd like them to be on my personal board of advisors. It elevates the relationship and heightens the possibility of meaningful value addition.

Over time, your advisory board can become a valuable network of trusted relationships that extends beyond professional advice, potentially leading to lifelong friendships and connections.

Personal Brand Tracking

Just as brands check in from time to time on their perceptions in the market, it makes sense for you to, once a year, step away from delivering your brand every day to take a temperature check of your progress in building Brand YOU.

Here is a lengthy checklist of things to think about that will help assess and track your personal brand equity:

- Are people aware of my personal brand?
- What is the perception of my personal brand among my target audience?
- How do they perceive my expertise, character and values?
- Is my brand associated with positive qualities and attributes?
- Am I consistently delivering on my brand promise?
- Are my actions and behaviours aligned with the values and messaging of my personal brand?
- Am I consistently providing value and delivering on expectations in my interactions and endeavours?
- What feedback have I received about my personal brand?
- Have I sought feedback from colleagues, peers, mentors or clients about their impressions of my brand?
- What have people said about their experiences with me and my work?
- Am I regarded as an authority or expert in my field?
- Have I made a positive impact within my industry or community?
- What are my online and offline brand touchpoints?
- Where and how is my personal brand being communicated, say, through LinkedIn, personal website, social media or public speaking engagements?

- How consistent is my branding across different platforms?
- Am I actively managing my online reputation?
- Have I conducted a regular online audit to ensure that search results and online profiles accurately reflect my personal brand?
- How do I handle online feedback and reviews, both positive and negative?
- What is the sentiment associated with my personal brand?
- Are mentions of my personal brand generally positive or negative in online conversations or reviews?
- How do people react to my brand on social media and other online platforms?
- Is my personal brand helping me achieve my goals?
- Have I set clear personal and professional goals for my brand, and am I making progress toward them?
- Can I attribute specific achievements or opportunities to my personal brand?
- Am I staying current and relevant in my field?
- Do I actively engage in continuous learning and professional development to stay up to date?
- Am I adapting to changes in my industry and incorporating relevant trends into my brand?
- How am I differentiating myself from competitors or peers?
- What sets me apart from others in my field or industry?
- Am I effectively communicating my unique value proposition?
- Are my personal brand metrics improving over time?
- Are my key performance indicators (KPIs) related to my personal brand (e.g., website traffic, social media engagement, speaking invitations) trending positively?
- Do I have a plan for addressing potential brand risks or crises?
- Have I identified potential risks to my personal brand, and do I have strategies in place to address them?

Regularly asking these questions and conducting brand assessments can help you gauge the health of your personal brand and make informed decisions about how to maintain and improve it. Consider creating a personal brand dashboard or scorecard to track relevant metrics and goals over time.

While this is not an easy task, it can be immensely valuable. Even if you don't create a dashboard, just reflecting on these questions can help you refine and evolve your personal brand strategy.

As we wrap up this section on promoting yourself, it's clear that developing a strong personal brand is not just an optional exercise but a crucial step in advancing your career. Through understanding the fundamental concepts of branding, appreciating its historical evolution, recognizing the significant edge it provides in today's competitive job market and learning about the systematic process to build your brand through the Five Acts of Building your Personal Brand, you are now well-prepared to embark on your personal branding journey.

Think carefully about whether you want to be intentional about building your personal brand or not. Once you decide to go for it, give it your 100 per cent. It will require time, energy and commitment. You will encounter setbacks at every step but reach out for help and keep persisting. Remember that the results won't be immediate. It will take a few years, if not longer, of consistent effort for you to build a personal brand that is recognised and sought after.

Most importantly, enjoy the journey. That itself is emotionally rewarding.

PART 3:

EVOLVE YOURSELF

IN PART 1 OF the book, I wrote about a holistic mind, body and soul approach to setting the foundation of your career.

In Part 2, I discussed the importance of building your personal brand and shared the five acts to help you discover, define, design, deploy and deliver your personal brand.

Part 3 involves thoughts for you on continuous growth and development paths that are essential for career acceleration. You must inculcate the mindset of always evolving yourself.

I discuss the things that you should commit to in the long term which will help position you as a distinguished professional who is not only highly successful in her career but has shaped the careers of many others, has contributed significantly to the organisation, has played a role in the industry and has positively contributed to society as well.

We'll talk about your commitment to evolving in three areas: (a)continuous growth and development, (b)helping others rise as you rise and (c)broadening your sphere of influence.

9

Continuous Growth and Development

Becoming a Lifelong Learner

I didn't embrace a lifelong-learner mindset well until I was mid-career. This is one of my biggest regrets because you never get back all the free time you had, especially in the earlier years of joining the workforce when there is relatively less stress and fewer responsibilities on the personal front.

The process of learning continues even after college is over. I had mistakenly equated the formal knowledge-gaining process in school and college with learning. While I had an open mind to learn on the job, I did not consciously seek out new areas for knowledge expansion and new skills that could benefit my growth.

When I look back, I was lucky that I managed to have some learning in spurts. I just had not managed to be systematic about it. And in hindsight, if I had pursued learning with more of a plan, I would be so much more of a learned person today.

A year after business school, I had six months of unemployment when I moved to California from India and was waiting for my H-4 employment visa to be processed. I was a young bride who had to set up and manage our first home. During this time, I taught myself to cook, something that I was severely anxious about. I surprised myself by how much I enjoyed learning to cook. Never having cooked a day in my life prior to this, suddenly I was able to effortlessly whip out dishes from comfort foods like rasam and sambhar to exotic ones like ratatouille and risotto.

My family and friends (especially those who don't have a knack for cooking) were surprised by how easily I taught myself to become a decent cook. All I was doing was reading recipes, getting a feel for the recipe in my mind in terms of the sequencing and then trying it out. It came naturally to me. Soon the kitchen was my playground, something I could have never imagined as I had absolutely no interest in the culinary world until then. I started avidly reading cookbooks. Soon my collection mushroomed, and I was teaching myself new cuisines, new ingredients and new techniques. I also started blogging at this time as a way of capturing my adventures with food! Blogging got me into writing regularly, a practice that would come handy years later.

During this same period when I had a lot of free time, I also started taking Spanish classes. One day when I was at the laundromat doing our laundry for the week, a middle-aged woman (who had probably just moved to Redwood City from Mexico) started talking to me in Spanish. I couldn't understand what exactly she was saying but I could tell she was struggling to use the washing machine and needed my help. I felt bad that I couldn't respond in Spanish. The language sounded so alluring. I went back to my apartment and started searching for Spanish classes. I had studied French in college, and I had heard that once you know one Romance language (a family of modern languages that evolved from Late Latin), picking up the others is relatively easier. While I studied Spanish for only three months during this period, I thoroughly enjoyed the process of learning a language again.

After my adventures with cooking and taking Spanish classes, there was a long period during which I didn't actively learn anything. I plunged into the world of work. I worked hard, giving my all to my job. I partied even harder. There was not much time left for any learning pursuits.

It was not until well into my mid-forties that I suddenly realised the need to keep seeking knowledge. This was triggered by one of Toddy Henry's books (I have read them all!) in which he recommends setting aside time to study something new every day. He suggests spending half your time absorbing the knowledge and half the time thinking about how best to apply it in your life. The second part is even more important than the first. We may take in a lot of knowledge but without a method to apply it, it's likely we won't retain much of it.

I reflected on Todd Henry's advice. I remembered my cooking and Spanish lessons and reminded myself of the joy I got from learning. I started thinking about all the avenues I could consciously learn from and the things I could do more of to become a lifelong learner.

Here are some of the things I started doing:

- Curating my reading list to include subjects I would normally not read
- Curating the podcasts I listen to by going far beyond business and marketing
- Reading magazines in new subject areas as diverse as astronomy and gardening
- Taking online courses (short and long)
- Signing up for workshops
- Going for industry events to learn more from practitioners

I also did a SWOT analysis (strengths, weaknesses, opportunities, threats) on myself to identify skills I could start learning before it was too late. Being digitally savvy was one of them; so I researched and paid for an online digital marketing certification.

What have I learned about incorporating learning into every day life?

Lifelong learning is a mindset. You must be conscious and embrace every opportunity to learn. It's not just about classes and courses.

Make dedicated time for learning. While we go about our lives being busy, if we don't carve out time for learning, precious years will be lost. Structure your time and schedule your learning sessions.

Make time for reflection and application. A lot of learning even from workshops and training sessions evaporates because we have not done the follow-up job of reflecting on what we have learned and how best to apply it. This is the most important aspect of learning.

Keep track of classes you've taken and new skills you have acquired. When you look back after five or ten years, this will be very helpful in remembering all that you invested in.

I recommend you organise all the information and store it physically or digitally so you can easily reference your past learning journey to support your career development. I have a physical folder in which I keep print outs of certificates of courses completed.

You can do this digitally as well. LinkedIn allows you to add certifications. Some people like to use educational tracking apps like Coursera. Even just keeping a note on a Spreadsheet, a Word document or your journal will suffice. Just write it down so you don't forget later!

Learning is a journey not a destination you reach after your graduation and post-graduation certificates have been awarded.

Humbition

As you grow in your career and become increasingly successful, one concept that can propel your growth as a leader even further is 'humbition'. Think of it as a blend of ambition and humility. Sanjiv Mehta, the former CEO of Hindustan Unilever in India, has popularised this term in India. He evangelises that the world needs more leaders who are hugely ambitious about the future and are extremely grounded.

The term 'humbition' has its roots in a study conducted by IBM to understand what sets high-impact employees apart. What emerged from the study is that ambition plus humility is a winning combination when it comes to the workplace. Jane Harper from the HR team at IBM coined this word while she was involved in a long-term endeavour on cultural transformation at the company.

Jane and her team created this guidance for leaders at IBM:

> 'We notice that by far the lion's share of world-changing luminaries are humble people. They focus on the work, not themselves. They seek success—they are ambitious—but they are humbled when it arrives. They know that much of that success was luck, timing, and a thousand factors out of their personal control. They feel lucky, not all-powerful. Oddly, the ones operating under a delusion that they are all-powerful are the ones who have yet to reach their potential... So be ambitious. Be a leader. But do not belittle others in your pursuit of your ambitions. Raise them up instead. The biggest leader is the one washing the feet of the others.'

As a leader you should see your primary goals as having a vision for the organisation, curating an all-star team and then helping everyone rise to their full potential.

'Helping others rise' became my mantra when I realised that being narcissistic, ego-centric and power hungry was not the kind of leader I wanted to be. One of my former bosses taught me that as a leader you should take all the blame when things go wrong and give all the credit to the team when things go well.

There are many ways to ensure you stay humble. They say that two things to remember are the bad we did to others and the good others did to us. Two things to forget are the good we've done for others and the bad that others have done to us.

Read that again. It is so simple and yet so powerful, isn't it? This truly puts things in perspective. We should remember our shortcomings and be grateful for what we received from others. Similarly, we should forgive and forget and not keep count of what we have done for others. In short, remembering your mistakes and forgetting your achievements allows you to stay grounded.

Listening intently is another way to stay humble and show deep respect. We have two ears and one mouth for a purpose. We need to listen more than we speak. Suspending our agenda, not planning what we will say next, truly being in the moment and tuning in to the other person's verbal and non-verbal cues is important to hear things others may miss.

Invite diverse perspectives. Sometimes we may be biased to think that only certain people produce brilliant ideas. The truth is hidden gems of insight can emerge from anyone if you only give them a chance. Be the person who invites others to contribute. Notice those whose voices are not being heard. Bring them in. Collaborate broadly.

Never act entitled. Don't command time, attention or respect just because you have a title. Entitlement is the antithesis of humility. Leadership is a responsibility and being a leader means you have to serve, not be served.

Use your achievements and experience to pass on knowledge to others. Put yourself in service of others in pursuit of collective ambition. That is the ultimate manifestation of humbition.

Swim in Your Own Lane

As the decibel levels on social media get louder each day, it is quite easy to feel inadequate unless you are absolutely secure in your sense of self and unaffected by braggadocio.

Across every sphere of your life someone in your social circle is inevitably achieving a whole lot more. Just take a moment to audit your feed across platforms. In a span of a few days you're likely to see everything – Matt's promotion to a challenging new role, Radhika's transformational weight loss journey, Alicia's cool videos of hot air ballooning with her besties in Cappadocia, Sunita raking up hundreds of likes and comments for a post on her fabulous workplace and Sumit's photos of him perfecting the Bhujangasana in addition to lots of cute baby, cat and dog videos and other bizarre content that pops up on your feed!

Add to this the fact that our social media consumption is rarely time bound. Open LinkedIn or Instagram and an hour later you might still be floating from one post to next, seamlessly aided by technology, hoping for some natural end which never comes.

This heady cocktail comes at an enormous price.

What is the knock off impact on your self-worth of your endless scrolling?

The infinite scroll is designed by Silicon Valley to be addictive for a reason. The term has transcended its original usage (easier pagination of content rather than clicking) to become a verb and a noun that has become, unfortunately, ubiquitous in our lives. More so for the young people around us.

If we're not careful, the infinite scroll could have a devastating effect on our productivity and creativity, not to mention physical and emotional wellbeing.

I am most worried about us getting distracted from achieving our goals because we see someone getting there faster or more easily or with less pain.

This is why it's critical to remember to swim in your own lane. If you look over to the right or the left, you're bound to lose focus and perhaps make a wrong move that will deny you victory.

The story of Chad Le Clos versus Michael Phelps, famous swimming rivals, in the 2016 Olympics 200m butterfly final is eye-opening. The South African youngster was all set to beat the American swimming legend. What was the result? Le Clos didn't beat Phelps. He didn't even get a medal. He finished fourth. Why? Photographs and video footage from the race show the exact moment at which Le Clos turned his head to look where Phelps was. That cost him dearly.

If we spend hours on end watching others achieve their goals, what happens to ours? We must stay absolutely grounded and focused on our purpose and our dreams and not allow distractions in any form, especially other people's achievements, to steer us off course.

It's not about always winning but rather giving everything our best efforts by having the right focus and direction.

Brands make this mistake as well. So often they are so worried about standing out from competitors that they forget that the real winner is the one who gets closest to the consumer.

There's no better way to becoming the best version of yourself than by remembering to swim in your own lane!

Louise Corbett, Leadership Coach, on swimming in your own lane

'Following your heart', 'listening to your intuition' or 'swimming in your own lane' can be terrifying, uplifting, intimidating, deeply rewarding and a journey that most won't ever endeavour but … I personally believe that it is only there that the universe truly has your back.

But first, you need to find out what your 'lane' is, and this can only really come from getting to understand the self and focusing on what really, truly (I mean at your deepest core) makes you feel like YOU.

On top of an unwavering dedication to turning down the volume on external expectations and finding the self, you also need to let go of the addiction to 'comparison'. Spending time on social media is OK but not beyond the point where it starts to make you feel less than (or before you know that feeling of lack is about to kick in). And in order to not be overtaken by the feeling of 'I'm not doing enough/I'm not achieving enough' try to constantly push yourself a little beyond your comfort zone. When we do that, we will also feel like we are 'going places' as, as they say 'Life begins on the other side of your comfort zone.'

Take it from someone who walked (overwhelmed by fear) the path of the unknown … you will never be the same again. It will be one of the most rewarding things you will ever do and … the universe will always have your back (just watch for the signs it will give you along the way).

The universe always rewards the brave.

Become a Great Listener

One of the things that I wish I had known when I started managing people is how very important listening is as a skill. We're not taught it at home, at school or even in college. We stumble into the workplace not realising how much we are lacking when it comes to listening skills. Yet, it is a critical skill when it comes to teamwork, collaboration and building relationships with co-workers all of which will play a role in your success. Especially as you grow in the ranks, the need for you to be an excellent listener becomes paramount.

As a new manager, I would get impatient when my team members were not listening to me. The penny only dropped many years later that I had to be an equally good listener and that listening was a great way to build rapport and trust with my team.

I also realised what a poor listener I was at home as a wife, as a mother and as a daughter. Endlessly distracted by my mobile phone and my overactive mind, was I truly listening to my husband's accounts of his day or my daughters' tales from school? Was I giving my parents my undivided attention, the only thing they truly cared about in their golden years? When I took a long hard look, and was honest with myself, the answer was that I was a very poor listener in all instances except when I was with my clients. With clients, somehow the adrenaline kicked in as I knew that I had to give them my 100 per cent to understand their needs and translate them effectively in the work we were doing for them. In front of clients, my distractions melted away. How do I channel my listening skills with clients to other areas of my life and improve my relationships?

As Amy Cuddy (social psychologist, best-selling author and TED speaker) rightly says: 'The paradox of listening is that when relinquishing power – the temporary power of speaking and asserting – we are acquiring power, the more lasting power of understanding and trusting.'

This rang so true with me. I was operating in the mode of speaking and asserting rather than active listening.

I learned to be a better listener from podcasts and books. What have I learned that I use every day? There are three levels of listening.

Level 1

The first level is when you are just hearing. You have to pay full attention to make sure you hear everything that is being said. You cannot be thinking about something else. You have to be fully focused and fully present.

Level 2

The second level is when you use empathy to understand where the other person is coming from. You're trying to get into the shoes of the person speaking in order to empathise with their feelings as much as you possibly can.

Level 3

The third and most important level is connecting with your feelings. What's going on inside you as you listen intently?

When you are fluent in all three levels of listening, you have developed a listening mindset, which makes you empathetic, curious and humble.

What are some other simple things you can do to be an active listener?

Make eye contact. However, if you keep staring it may be intimidating for the other person. Break eye contact every ten seconds or so and then redirect.

Have an open stance. Having crossed arms when conversing with someone (which I used to be so guilty of!) can come across as defensive. It can leave an unfavourable impression.

Stay present in the conversation. Put away all distractions, especially the mobile phone. Work hard to not let your mind run away to something else. If it does, bring it back to the present conversation. Resist the urge to frame your responses to what the other person is saying.

Play back what is being said. Say it a few times. Ask the speaker to ensure that you have captured what they have said fully. At the end, ask if the other person has more to say. Give them a few chances to come out with everything. Then you can paraphrase and summarise. Preferably use their words not yours. This is key to listening as it validates the speaker that they are being heard and understood. It's equally important to nod and give the other person an indication to show you are listening.

Don't interrupt. I used to be a flagrant interrupter until I realised how terrible the practice is. It is rude and disrespectful. You have to be patient and allow the other person to speak even if they are slow. If there are moments of silence, let the awkward moment be. Don't rush in to fill the silence with your words.

Actively look for non-verbal cues beyond the words. Be a good judge of body language. What are the eyes, the expressions, the body saying that the words are not?

Ask questions to understand better what is being said. Questions are a good way to crowd out judgement and to stay curious about what you are hearing. Open-ended questions are better than closed ones. For example, don't say, 'Did my actions upset you?' That will give you a binary answer, which is not particularly helpful. Rather if you ask, 'What actions of mine were the most hurtful?', you will get a much richer response.

These are just a few of the techniques that have worked for me. While I've improved massively, I still have a long way to go. Not only do I have to work hard to block out distractions, but I also have to constantly remind myself to not jump in and respond, be judgemental or interrupt just to get it over with rather than seeking to understand the other person.

As your professional commitments and stress levels increase, the harder it becomes to be a good listener. The only way is to be fully conscious and switched on to active listening mode when the situation demands. The good news is that as with all things, practice helps you get better. The benefits are immediate and don't take long to accrue. The best reward is the strengthening of your relationships at work and at home.

Negotiation

You'll be surprised how handy good negotiation skills are in the workplace. The application of negotiation is far more common than you think – it's not just reserved for the realm of high-stake sales and performance appraisals. Negotiation can be useful in everyday activities.

You need negotiation skills to manage your workload with your boss. You need them to coax more out of your co-workers and direct reports. You need them to sell ideas. You need them when you must convince someone not to quit your organisation. You need them to convince your team about your idea for the office outing. So many situations in which it would be so handy to be able to get your way!

At its core, negotiation is a game of emotions. If you don't have high emotional intelligence, you're likely to be a weak negotiator. Why? Because you must be aware of your own emotions and those of others' to come out the winner in a negotiation.

When I reflect on situations where I didn't negotiate well, there are some common themes. My ego had gotten in the way. I was thinking more about what I wanted to achieve than trying to understand the other person. I wasn't really listening to what they were saying because I was eagerly waiting to get my word in every time I had a chance. I underestimated how much the other person wanted something and would have done anything to not let go of what they wanted.

Over the years, I've learned that communication and negotiation are intrinsically linked. Negotiation is as much about empathy, listening, openness, warmth and care as it is about confidence, clarity, coherence and articulation.

You need to have an investigative mindset to uncover the truth of what the other person wants and then use all the tools in your toolkit to create a win for both parties. I learned this and many more insights from Chris Voss's book *Never Split the Difference: Negotiating as if Your Life Depended on It*, which is considered the best book by far on the topic.

Here are some handy tips to use during negotiations:

- Do your homework about the other person – who they are (use the Internet, speak to others) as well as what they may really want in the situation.
- Keep an open mind as you enter the discussion. Your stand could change after you learn more about their needs. You may get less than what you asked for. Be prepared to compromise.
- Listen attentively. Look for verbal and non-verbal cues. Get out of your head and into theirs.
- Create a common ground. Try to create a genuine connection before you start negotiating.
- Try mirroring to build rapport. Every few minutes make sure you play back what they've said. You can even nod along and mirror other physical gestures. (A study showed that waiters who mirrored their guests were tipped 70 per cent more than on occasions when they didn't mirror their guests.)
- Tune in to emotions more than logic– both yours and theirs.
- Always ask for what you want. Don't shy away. The worst thing that can happen is you'll hear a no.
- Also, ask for more than what you expect to get and you'll be surprised at what you receive.
- Know when to walk away. Don't give everything away if it doesn't match with your values.
- Sometimes no can be the most powerful word.
- Before the discussion ends, restate the agreement and seek confirmation.

10

Helping Others Rise as You Rise

Celebrating Others

'Promise yourself today to be just as enthusiastic about the success of others as you are about your own,' said Christian D. Larson.

There's no better way to deepen relationships than by genuinely celebrating others. This requires us to step out of the narcissistic bubble we may unconsciously be wrapping ourselves in.

Many famous people prioritise celebrating others. Oprah is known for her generosity and for celebrating the achievements of others. She has often used her platform to uplift and highlight the work of others from authors to activists to everyday people making a difference in their communities. Her book club has changed the fortunes of unknown authors.

Taylor Swift is lauded for being supportive of her fans and fellow musicians. She frequently interacts with fans on social media and has been known to surprise them with gifts and personal messages.

Richard Branson is often seen celebrating the successes of his employees and colleagues, and he is known for being approachable and encouraging.

Arianna Huffington has spoken about the importance of celebrating small wins and creating a culture of appreciation and recognition in the workplace.

On a recent birthday, I analysed how each message, each gift, each call from my family and friends made me feel. What did I conclude? When the other person is genuinely celebrating me, I feel it so clearly, and it certainly draws me closer to them. When you put time, thought and effort, it shows. It made me realise how important it is to take time out from our busy schedules to celebrate others and celebrate them more often.

What are some of the ways in which you can celebrate others?

Say it with words. There is nothing better than walking up to someone and expressing your appreciation, congratulations or gratitude. So easy to do, isn't it? Just walk around your office or home and find a way to do this more often. Even better if you can add an element of physical touch (with due caution of course). It's so rewarding to lighten up others!

Send a thoughtful message. I really miss old-fashioned paper cards. The best way to share a thoughtful message is to pick out the right card and pen a few words. You can use a user-friendly online design platform like Canva to design a digital card. Also, just a few words on text, with or without emojis, would work well. The important bit is to consider and customise what you want to say and how you want to make the other person feel. Don't bother to send out a hurried 'Happy Birthday!' or 'Congrats!' to tick the box. Nothing screams lack of care more than a generic message like that. Address the person by their name and write a few sentences for them. Infuse the message with warmth and care.

Give a gift. For the special relationships, make an extra effort to send something. It is easy to order flowers online no matter which city people live in. Within the same city, of course, the choices are endless. Many of the e-commerce brands like Amazon and Tata Cliq Luxury make gift certificates very easily. Gift certificates for day spas or home spas are increasing in popularity as well. A personalised gift is the most special. An intern of ours crocheted me an exquisite purse and gifted it to me when her internship ended. That purse and the beautiful sentiments expressed in a handwritten card are among my cherished possessions.

Host a celebration. When you want to kick it up a notch, host a celebration! Throw a birthday party. Host a baby shower. Organise a group getaway to celebrate a friend's success. The possibilities are many. The generosity and effort you put into hosting a celebration like this for someone special can go a long way in deepening your relationship.

Share their success on social media. You may be posting birthday wishes for friends and colleagues on social media, but can you take to it more often to celebrate their achievements as well? Assuming they are fine with it of course. I would like to try more often to celebrate those in my network.

Make time. Often, the biggest gift you can give is the gift of your time, your attention and love. If you have to prioritise one way of celebrating others, make it this one.

Celebrating others is all about showing appreciation and recognition for their accomplishments and contributions. Find a way that feels authentic and meaningful to you, and the recipient is sure to feel valued and appreciated.

Celebrating others is a powerful way to build relationships, boost morale, spread positivity and encourage collaboration. It's a simple yet impactful way to show appreciation and support for those around us.

Managing Comparison

In *Atlas of the Heart*, Brene Brown talks about the emotional places we go when we compare: admiration, reverence, envy, jealousy, resentment, schadenfreude, freudenfreude. I could relate to it as I've had at least a few conversations in the past few weeks with my daughters and a few colleagues on the importance of swimming in your own lane, because if you don't, then you end up feeling so many complicated emotions that negatively impact your self-worth.

Research tells us that comparing ourselves with others is 'a pervasive social phenomenon' and 'our sense of where we stand impacts our self-concept, our level of aspiration and our overall well-being.'

How can we unshackle ourselves from the tyranny of self-comparison to lead happier and more fulfilling lives?

I find these four suggestions on managing comparison from *Coach on the Go* very practical:

- Admiration – look at the person you are comparing yourself to and find inspiration.
- Watch how much time you spend on social media. Get out and live your life instead.

- Freudenfreude – focus on celebrating the success of others instead of comparing. Lift each other up.
- Practice self-compassion when comparison shows up. Loving and belonging to yourself is key.

In a paper in the World Journal of Psychiatry and Mental Health Research, Brene gives us two additional practical behaviours to practice.

Shoy

'Shoy' is the term to describe the act of intentionally sharing the joy of someone relating a success story by showing interest and asking follow-up questions. While I do my best to genuinely feel the other person's success, what I will do more is ask better follow-up questions to understand their success better. I am sure this will help in cultivating a deeper relationship.

Bragitude

'Bragitude' refers to intentionally tying words of gratitude toward the listener following discussion of personal success. Rather than being embarrassed by words of praise or congratulations, I am going to be genuinely grateful for the joy in my success that the other person is expressing.

We may be subconsciously ruining our days by being on the treadmill of comparison. It not only robs us of joy every day but can have a devastating outcome leaving us despondent if we don't regulate our emotions. The key is self-awareness which can then lead to slowly shedding these negative emotions.

Leading with Compassion

As you grow in your career, how you shape yourself as a leader will have a big impact on how you are perceived. Even if you don't have a C-Suite or senior management leadership title, you can apply these principles to be more effective in leading others.

Place others' interest over self-interest

The biggest mindset shift to make when you move from individual contributor to leader is that you have to put the interest of others first. I'm reminded of a line from the school song we sang every day in high school: 'School first, House next, self last.' Whether it is your organisation, your business unit, your team or some other unit, start by putting their interests over yours. For example, if you're given an opportunity to speak at an event, consider how this will be good for the organisation and not just your career. If one of your team members says she is quitting as she got a better job, can you be genuinely excited for what might be progress for her rather than immediately thinking about what impact her quitting would have on your workload? Every day you will encounter situations in which you will be tested. Leaders who are not self-centred will ensure that they don't judge every situation through the prism of their own lens. You should keep asking yourself how your actions will help others.

Put yourself in their shoes

A corollary to the above principle is to imagine what the other person is thinking and feeling. It's all about empathy. In the busyness of the workplace, empathy is far easier said than done, but good leaders remind themselves that what matters is how aware they are to the emotions of their employees.

Walk the halls, observe others and develop a sensitive radar so you can pick up on non-verbal cues in team meetings and one-on-one conversations. Know as much as you can about the full backgrounds of your team members. Have regular check-ins so you are updated on their personal lives as well to the extent they are willing to share.

All of this allows a better understanding of what people are going through and hence the sensitivity with which you have to conduct your conversations. This does not mean that you would avoid tough conversations with those who may be going through difficulty outside of work. We all have things we are dealing with personally which may cause our emotions to go on a rollercoaster ride. Despite that, at work we have to show up and be a thorough professional. Just apply extra layers of sensitivity to the conversation so that you don't diminish the individual's sense of self-worth. When I was new to my leadership role, I made many mistakes in this regard. I would be quite stern with feedback thinking I was just doing my duty to ensure the work was of the highest quality. I didn't pay as much attention to how my feedback impacted the individual who had created the work. What a huge mistake! We have to care about the individual as much as we do about the work.

Be sincere and generous with praise and gratitude

One of the easiest ways to lift others up is to actively find opportunities to praise your colleagues and to be grateful for their contributions. Everyone craves validation and recognition no matter how senior they are. The key is to be sincere when you dole out appreciation.

After a good meeting, pull someone aside and give them a pat on the shoulder for a job well done. Be specific with your praise. You could say, for example, that the way they explained the idea was particularly inspiring. Or the way they responded to a tough question showed how well prepared the team was. When praise is specific, it is much more effective.

Find ways to thank your colleagues. This could be relayed verbally after a job well done or via quick email or text. Recognising the time and effort people put into projects and tasks is a great way of signalling you have noticed their contributions. Tell people why the work they do matters and how it makes a positive contribution to the organisation.

Don't be afraid of overdoing it. Leaders don't praise enough. No matter how much you already do, it is perhaps not enough for your team.

Be that leader who treats everyone decently day in and day out and who goes out of their way to recognise others.

Make time

To lead with compassion, you have to intimately know the people you are leading. This requires time and energy in getting to know the key people on the team. This may require an initial meeting to get an overview of their backgrounds and history at the company as well as their personal lives.

Regular check-ins with direct reports are required to signal you care about their progress and want to help them accomplish more. The cadence of your check-ins is also important. Too often and you may be seen as a leader who micromanages. Too few and you may be seen as not caring enough about your direct reports.

For example, when I was Managing Director of Landor, India, I did a weekly check-in with everyone on my leadership team, but after I took on the Vice President of APAC role, I had to think of a lesser frequency of check-ins be able to cover my team in all the other markets. Sometimes these less frequent meetings would get skipped due to a busy schedule but I could immediately see the negative consequences of not speaking to my direct reports for more than a month.

You have to prioritise your time for your team.

Have a 360-degree view on all stakeholders

Leaders have to not only worry about understanding and empathising with their internal stakeholders but have to broaden this understanding for all stakeholders in their ecosystem. It could include clients, partners, vendors, agencies, regulators and society at large. To lead with compassion, you must be in touch with the stated and unstated needs of these different stakeholders and how this impacts the organisation. This information will be critical in helping you make the right decisions for your company while balancing the needs of other stakeholders.

For example, at Landor, we often get complaints from freelancers about late payments. We can either blame this on internal financial processes and ask them to deal with the delays if they wish to continue to work with us. Or we can be empathetic and compassionate towards the cash flow needs of individuals who deliver high quality work for us and hence redesign our freelancer payment system to ensure that they are paid in a timely manner.

As you grow as a leader, the number of different stakeholder groups you have to manage will only increase. Developing mutual understanding and trust with these different groups will be key to your success. This is especially important if you rise to becoming the CEO of your company. Today, companies are not only measured by the amount of shareholder wealth they create but by how they manage all stakeholders.

Mentoring

Mentoring is a mindset. Think of it as helping others to rise. When someone mentors you, they help you to rise. When you mentor someone, you are helping them to rise.

How do you help others rise? It's through a combination of knowledge dissemination, experience sharing, advice and active help such as facilitating introductions to expand their network.

Wherever in your career you are, I would strongly recommend getting a mentor or two in addition to mentoring one or two juniors yourself.

When you are both a mentee (recipient) as well as a mentor (giver), the benefit is tremendous. I've operated this way for years and find that the overall exchange of ideas and useful guidance has a positive domino effect on everyone involved.

Experienced people benefit from reverse mentoring and receiving ideas from junior colleagues in their fields. On the other hand, younger people benefit from the wisdom of the more experienced ones.

For example, it was from an intern that I learned about leap.club, a private network for women and then applied to become a member. Had it not been for my conversation with my young mentor, I would not have ever heard of this wonderful organisation. In turn, I have introduced leap.club to so many of my mentees who have benefited from the club's services to its members. One of my mentors told me early on that it was critically important to learn the language of the boardroom to be effective in it while making high-stakes presentations. This advice I pass on to my mentees so they can train themselves from a young age on things that matter to the board of directors of a company.

Mentoring opens your mind in ways that books, podcasts and videos do not. As you develop a relationship with your mentor, they get to know you more intimately and can offer tailored guidance, which can be more beneficial than pure self-help.

Mentors can help you develop hard skills required for technical competence as well as soft skills needed for leadership advancement. I had a mentor in brand strategy who I used to have a weekly lunch with during my tenure at Landor in San

Francisco. The things I picked up informally over our lunch dates were more valuable than any formal training could have ever provided. Soft skills are harder to learn from conversations. They are better learned by observing others in action and assimilation. Early in your career, you should try to get as much exposure as you can to the seniors in your company so you can watch how they operate and emulate them.

Some companies have professional career advancement programmes. In others, you have to muddle your way through. This is where a mentor can provide guidance about career paths, possible next roles, how to ask for what you deserve and so on.

Another benefit of mentoring is in its ability to help you expand your network. Mentors can introduce mentees to valuable contacts in and outside of their industry, expanding their professional network.

If you are a young woman leader, you can take advantage of a mentor who is a senior woman leader. She would have experienced similar challenges as you have and there will be valuable lessons for you. Her career journey and choices in themselves could be inspiration for you. You can share gender-specific challenges more easily and be open about your vulnerabilities.

While mentorship programs may have a fixed duration, think of these as long-lasting relationships that you want to sustain for life. That's the mentality with which you should approach these mentorship opportunities. The more you invest, the more you will get out of them.

One of the biggest satisfactions I have had in my professional career is having mentored hundreds of young men and women over the last two decades. I am particularly proud of having been a founding member of WPP Stella India, a mentorship programme for high-potential women in WPP companies. WPP is a multinational communications, advertising, public relations, technology and commerce company.

Set up around five years ago, WPP Stella India is a structured approach to mentoring wherein programme members get paired with a senior woman mentor from a different operating company to theirs in the group. You are either nominated by your company or you can apply yourself to be a part of the programme. In addition to monthly sessions with your mentor, you also get access to educational, up-skilling and inspirational sessions. More than three hundred women have successfully completed at least one year of mentoring. I've mentored four women through the programme who I am still very much in touch with.

11

Broadening Your Influence

As you become more senior, you have to carve out more time to participate and add value outside of the company you work for. This will not only broaden your network but will also add to your professional achievements while giving you meaningful pursuits.

While you can start giving back at any age, once you hit the Director level, you should be actively looking for opportunities to contribute to the world that exists outside the company.

Industry Events

The lowest-hanging fruit is industry events. Most industries have an industry body as well as other organisations that organise events at which people from the industry regularly gather for learning, inspiration, rewards and recognition.

The advertising, media and marketing industry in India, for example, has The Advertising Club, The Effies, Kyoorius Awards, GoaFest, Kyoorius DesignYatra and Smarties to name just a few.

You can look for speaking slots or be on the jury for awards. You can join the management committee of one of your industry bodies or you can simply start by showing up at the events hoping to meet like-minded people. You never know where chance meetings with key people might take you.

Make the time in your busy schedule to attend industry events. You need to be visibly seen as an active participant who is contributing to your industry.

Corporate Boards

In India, there are now mandatory guidelines around having women on corporate boards. This is a great opportunity to contribute and build your profile.

One of the best ways to become eligible for corporate boards is to get certified to be an independent director. Do take the course offered by a reputed institute so that you know all the risks involved with such a role. This is not a must have in order to be on a board but it will prepare you well.

You can either be proactive in your outreach or wait for companies to approach you. It usually happens through informal networking and word of mouth. Make sure you maintain a highly credible professional reputation and have built equity in a particular industry or area of expertise.

Corporate boards are demanding. To contribute well, you have to do the prep work. Don't commit if you don't have the time but if you do consider becoming a board member, it can greatly enhance your profile and accelerate your career.

Nonprofits

Nonprofits in our country are desperate for talented individuals who can contribute with their knowledge, skills and connections. While the non-profit sector may not be your calling, you can make a difference by joining the advisory board of a non-profit, consulting for free or simply volunteering to start with.

There are many nonprofits serving a range of different audiences in India. Pick an organisation whose mission you are passionate about. Do your research about the non-profit. Look in your network for who can connect you and make the move.

Being part of a non-profit will be a standout in your profile. It shows you are a leader who uses her time and talent to contribute to important causes.

Part 4:

Handy How-Tos

Think of this part as a practical playbook dedicated to equipping you with the indispensable skills for navigating the intricate terrain of your career journey.

Here I dive into a series of how-tos, each designed to empower you with actionable insights and strategies. Whether you're aiming to negotiate a well-deserved raise, master the art of acing job interviews or gracefully assert yourself by saying no, these practical tips are tailored to elevate your professional prowess.

Discover the art of articulating your value and negotiating for your worth with 'How to Ask for a Raise'. Navigate the daunting realm of job interviews with confidence, armed with the tactics outlined in 'How to Ace a Job Interview'. Learn the power of setting boundaries and reclaiming control over your time and priorities in 'How to Say No'.

Building a supportive network is crucial, and in 'How to Build a Tribe', I walk you through the steps of cultivating meaningful professional connections. Find your voice and express dissent constructively in 'How to Disagree with Bosses and Colleagues', a skill that is crucial in fostering a dynamic and inclusive workplace.

Unlock the secrets of persuasive communication with 'How to Ask for Anything', embrace resilience with grace in 'How to Handle Rejection' and prepare for a mindset shift with 'How to Overcome Internal Barriers to Success'.

Each how-to is a tool in your kit, a compass guiding you through the nuances of professional life.

As you embark on this journey of self-empowerment, remember that mastering these how-tos is not just about surviving but thriving. Let these practical insights be your companion as you navigate the twists and turns of your career path, armed with the knowledge and confidence to excel in every professional endeavour. Ace these and you will be well on your way to going further, faster.

Asha Kharga, Chief Customer and Brand Officer at the Mahindra Group, shares insights on 'Embracing Career Clarity: 10 Truths to Guide You'.

1. Grit is the secret weapon for success. Grit turns setbacks into comebacks.
2. Own your story, be your biggest cheerleader and avoid comparisons. Your journey is unique – celebrate it proudly.
3. One invaluable piece of advice I have received is to treat your current role as the best job in the world. Amid the constant anticipation for the next step or promotion, it's easy to lose sight of the present and, if things don't unfold as expected, succumb to bitterness. Instead, immerse yourself in the present work, embrace it wholeheartedly – it's in this immersion that true fulfilment and success often blossom.
4. The average career is close to a 40-year journey filled with unexpected twists – roles not panning out, promotions that elude you, encounters with challenging bosses or toxic work cultures – yet life has a natural rhythm. What descends will inevitably rise. A couple of challenging years are fleeting moments, not defining chapters.
5. Be a doer. Always.
6. Invest in meaningful connections with people; their true worth shines especially when there are differing opinions. When there is a strong foundation of trust and understanding in relationships, it becomes easier to navigate and resolve disagreements. This is true for work and for life.
7. Be a mentor. Have a reverse mentor.
8. Accept the reality of work–life integration; acknowledge that weekends may include work and seek an organisation that supports you when life demands attention during the week.

9. Be intentional about making time for deep thinking. Find your rituals around it – waking up early in the morning, not checking the mobile immediately and organising the day can set a positive tone for the day ahead.
10. Embrace feedback. It is a gift.

How to Ask for a Raise

A Glassdoor survey in India found that one-third of women never ask for a raise at work and a staggering 68 per cent do not negotiate pay when offered a job. Often, women are unsure of their abilities to negotiate, unsure of the value they bring to the table or do not want to come across as aggressive and worry about the impact that such conversations could have on their relationships with their bosses. Many of us don't like to have uncomfortable conversations. However, if you don't get the salary that you deserve at every level of your career, you will be behind in your professional journey, and it will be difficult to catch-up in later years.

The first step in asking for a raise is to do a self-assessment. Evaluate your performance against the goals and KPIs that you have been given. If you don't have formal objectives, write down what your boss expects of you and gauge your progress against those expectations. Make a list of your contributions to the organisation. Collect and document all your evidence. Proof points are important. If you have done well, you and your manager will be surprised by how much you have achieved when you put it all down. It is equally important to back off from asking for a raise if your assessment shows that you may not have achieved the objectives and have less tangible proof. Be honest with yourself at this stage. Is this an emotional need or is it truly deserved based on your contribution to the company's objectives?

Next, research the salary bands for your level by speaking to your friends in your industry and other industries. Develop relationships with key recruiters who may also be able to give you this information. These recruiter relationships will also be useful at other times in your professional career.

Speak to colleagues internally and determine the right time to ask for a raise. Some companies will have formal periods during which it is acceptable to have these conversations. In companies where there is a less formal approach, you must choose the right time to have the conversation. Never have the conversation more than once a year. Don't have it when the company is not doing well or when it is a stressful time for your boss. The ideal time is a month or two before your formal raise cycle/increment period. Choose a day a few weeks after you may have accomplished something and you'll have some immediate leverage in the conversation, however small that may be.

Make sure you have prepared your 'stump speech' on why you deserve a raise. Keep it short and matter of fact. Reinforce your commitment to the company's growth. Show you are invested in the company. Showcase your achievements verbally. You can give a handout with bullet points. Having done your research, state your expectation on your raise. Don't fall into the trap of comparing yourself to X or Y in your company. Focus on your achievements and your expectations based on your research and your contributions.

Make sure you practise by role-playing with a friend before you have the conversation with your boss.

When you have the meeting to ask for your raise, be professional and confident. Self-belief is key here. Dress well and feel good about yourself. At the same time don't be so focused on your own agenda that you forget to listen to your boss's response. Practise active listening and play back what he or she says to make sure you have understood it.

You may get an immediate response. If it's a yes, be sure to say thank you and reinforce your commitment to the company's growth. If it's a no, try to understand what more your boss expects you to do to be worthy of a raise. Understand the expectations from his or her perspective as objectively as you can. It is best not to respond immediately. Ask for a follow-up meeting on this once you have had a chance to recalibrate your thoughts.

If you get a promise for future consideration, say thank you and ask for a specific timeframe for the reconsideration. While you should not threaten that you might leave, you should give a sense of not being happy with the decision and that you may explore other opportunities.

The objective of having this meeting to ask for a raise is to clearly signal that you know your value, you expect the organisation to match your needs and that you may consider other opportunities if the needs are not met.

What is the worst-case scenario that speaking up and having this conversation can result in? You may not get exactly what you asked for, but you may get some portion of it. Even that is progress.

If your request for a raise is ignored and you are not satisfied with the justification, it is time to seriously evaluate your options. Don't be stuck working for a company that does not value your contributions. You have more options than you think. Start actively exploring how you might advance your career elsewhere.

This is why it's all the more important to invest in your personal brand as it gives you more negotiation power and can help you command a premium in the talent market.

I encounter these conversations at work every year. I've seen some people do it the correct way and others be aggressive and demand raises without having contributed. Last year, I was particularly impressed by one young woman on our team who did an excellent job of the conversation with me asking for a raise. She had prepared a printed document in which she had listed her contributions to the company in the form of outcomes delivered; not only what she had done but the value it contributed. She had compiled some feedback from clients in the form of client quotes and included this in the pack as well. She prepared well for the conversation, and during the chat itself, she laid it all out and was confidently assertive but not threatening. She was relaxed and confident, making the best case for herself as she could. All these factors led me to give her a healthy raise that year.

How to Ace a Job Interview

Most companies are not looking to just fill vacant positions. They are desperate for qualified candidates who not only meet the technical skills but are earnest, enthusiastic, passionate, hardworking and invested in the company's growth.

Beyond technical skills tests which I cannot prepare you for, there are things that I would recommend you do which will put you ahead of others. These are not difficult to do, but they require time and effort. Surprisingly, many candidates do not bother with these so if you do them you will certainly benefit.

It all comes down to one word: preparation.

Prep. Prep. Prep.

Research the company thoroughly. Read the website – every word on it. Download the annual reports. Read as many of them as you can. Get a sense of the company's vision and values. Understand its performance holistically, not only its financials. What is the company's environmental, social and governance record? Who are the leaders? Do they have strong profiles in the industry? What is the future of the company? What is the future of the business unit/department/role you are applying for? Are there any misdeeds of the company you should be aware of?

Get a sense of the culture. Read reviews on Glassdoor. Try to speak with current and former employees informally. Ask friends for introductions, failing which write some cold call messages on LinkedIn to reach people who can give you feedback on the culture. Very often you tend to neglect bad comments on a company's culture when focused on landing a job, but it is much worse to have a job and be stuck in a bad culture than not have a job at all. Equally, do not be overly influenced by a few negative comments written by disgruntled employees. Having a balanced view is necessary.

Thoroughly research the people you will be interviewing with. Make sure you know their profiles and read everything about them you can find online. If you know people who know them, reach out to them with a message via your contact that you are keen on the company and that your contact would personally recommend you for the role.

Spend time dissecting the job description of the role you are applying for. What do you bring to the table that others won't? What unique experiences make you the ideal candidate? What past experiences lend themselves perfectly to this one? Anticipate all the questions that the interviewer might ask you and think through your responses. Have a battery of stories you can draw up of your achievements, failures and learnings from previous roles.

Do some mock interviews with friends or well-wishers so you can practise your answers and develop greater confidence.

Plan your attire based on the typical dress code of the company. Aim for one level smarter. For example, if employees usually wear jeans and t-shirts with sneakers, perhaps you can go in for jeans, a blazer with a smart blouse and formal shoes.

On D-Day, dress well and carry your confidence proudly. Make sure you arrive well ahead of time to avoid any last-minute stress from travel.

The first eye contact is important. Smile and be relaxed, not too nervous and not too casual. Give a firm handshake that expresses your confidence and comfort.

Don't be in a rush to oversell yourself by speaking too much. Listen carefully to the questions being asked and respond thoughtfully. Show genuine interest in the interviewer(s). Keep your answers precise, illustrate with examples and showcase your passion and enthusiasm for the role. Articulate your achievements clearly. When asked tricky questions, be as honest as possible while sharing your learnings (in case of failures).

Sit straight, don't play with your hair or nails. Don't be distracted by your mobile phone. Put it on silent and tuck it away in your handbag. Positive and professional body language is important.

Pepper in as much of the company and interviewer research you did as relevant – don't do it to show off how much research you have done but only where it genuinely adds value to the conversation. Demonstrate genuine knowledge about the company and the requirements of the role. Assure the interviewer of your commitment to achieving goals, working hard, being a team player and a good corporate citizen. Be prepared to ask questions if you have the opportunity.

After the interview, send a follow-up thank you note. Attach any additional work samples or references that may be relevant. If you don't hear back, follow up to inquire about the status of your application. When you get a rejection letter, don't go silent. Write back acknowledging the opportunity you had, expressing disappointment that you didn't get the role and stating your desire to stay in touch for possible future opportunities.

From personal experience, the two things that are most critical are the preparation for the interview and the follow-up post the interview. Both can help you create a profile that stands out in the crowded marketplace.

I remember the candidates who thoroughly researched the company and me (the person they are interviewing with). It helps to make a positive impression when you can confidently talk about the strategy of the company and its competitors as you have done the prep. One person who was interviewing with me for a strategist position claimed that he had read every piece of information on the Internet about the company and me. It was a tall claim, but he came through very well when I tested him.

Sending a thank you note after an interview seems like good etiquette but less than 1 per cent of candidates do it. It's a nice way to follow up and stay in touch and reinforce what you bring to the table and your interest in the company. A few months ago, a senior client director I was interviewing sent a thorough follow-up or thank-you note. It helped me recall all the value this candidate was going to bring to us.

This is one area in your life in which you should not take any shortcuts.

How to Say No

When you are in the early stages of your career, you may feel you can never say no to anything asked of you at work lest that be a career-limiting move. However, there are times when you must learn to say no to protect your mental, physical and emotional wellbeing.

Manage your workload

Say no to additional assignments when you are already overloaded. Only you can accurately assess your workload. Only you know how much you have on your plate and how much more you can take on or not. Others who are delegating tasks to you seldom have the full picture. Of course, you should be working to full capacity before saying no and not be declining requests when you are only at half or three-fourths capacity, but when you are close to 100 per cent, a clear no is better than a weak yes that will break the camel's back.

How do you respectfully push back? I have learned to say that I would love to help but need guidance on prioritising the tasks on my plate. Something will have to be moved for me to take on something more. A few things happen when I am transparent .The person asking me to do something may back off because they can see I am at full capacity. Or the person may help me delegate one of my tasks to make room for the new one or help me deprioritise another. Having the courage to have these conversations regularly can prevent burnout.

Prioritise your tasks

Say no to extra responsibilities at work that may take away from the focus on your goals. Of course, you should do some pro bono work. Of course, you should be part of the culture task force. Of course, you should volunteer to organise fun events and other things like that. But too many of these extras on your plate will come in the way of you achieving your goals. Don't say yes to every single one of these. Choose a few that give you joy and say no to the rest.

Maintain your integrity

Say no to gossiping about others. Many times, you will be in a situation where people would be talking ill of colleagues. Resist the temptation to join the conversation.You don't want to inadvertently contribute to the conversation by sharing trusted information about others or speaking ill of someone when they are not around. It's best to leave the room or just say you would not like to participate.

Maintain boundaries

Say no to going out with a colleague who asks you out if you are not comfortable, even if it is your boss or a senior colleague. Don't feel professionally obliged.

Here are a few things to keep in mind:

Listen empathetically and hear the person out fully before you say no. You want to give the assurance that you have carefully considered the request.

Practice saying no in the nicest manner possible. Be clear and direct – no need to beat around the bush. Get straight to the point. When I say no, I try to offer alternate solutions when relevant.

Don't feel guilty after saying no. Stay the course and learn to manage your feelings.

Don't give in to pressure by the one making the request. Stay calm and composed while maintaining your stance.

Don't feel like you need to excessively apologise for saying no. It's acceptable. While it is good to give a reason why you are saying no, it is not necessary.

Saying no is like a muscle you need to develop. The more you say it, the better you will get at it.

How to Build a Tribe

I have always envied my friends who have a group of very close friends that have stayed together for decades. I moved schools many times when I was younger. I did my undergrad in the US and my postgrad in India. This constant movement of location did not allow me to build a tribe of friends as much as I would've liked to have.

So how do you build a tribe if you don't have one from your childhood or college days?

Common interests are one great way. Look for groups that share your passions. If you can't find any, create your own!

I joined a book club three years ago. It is called The Deep Dive Business Book Club. Fifteen of us came together three years ago and have stayed together since (on a WhatsApp group and Zoom for our monthly meetings). We bond through the books we read and the topics and sub-topics they lead us to. Some of us are new moms, others empty nesters. The friendship across generations binds us even more strongly. I may not have time to read a book each time, but I make it a point to join as many of the book club meetings as I can to keep in touch with the group. We have had several in-person meetings over the years and would love to do more. Even though we aren't the closest of friends, I would say this is my tribe.

One of my friends has a group in her building who play volleyball together. They have formed a club and compete against other clubs. This is a great way to get in exercise and have your sporting tribe.

Another friend loves to sketch. Once, she chose 9 a.m. on Sunday mornings in Mumbai to go to different architectural monuments each week in the city and sketch for a few hours. She started an Instagram page and invited others to join. Her sketching tribe has now grown leaps and bounds and is a veritable community of enthusiasts.

Someone I know hated reading the news because of the poor quality of the reporting. So she decided to start an everyday newsletter to change how we consume news. She collated the day's news, picked a lead story, summarised it in easy to digest language and started publishing every day. The group has expanded exponentially and was a lifeline for many during Covid-19.

You can start a tribe too. With WhatsApp and social media, it is easier than ever to create a group around shared interests, values and passions. Think about what most excites you and what you want to pursue as a hobby. Create a name for your group, write out your purpose/vision/mission, set up a website/ Facebook page/WhatsApp group and get going! Before you know it, your tribe will organically grow.

You have to stay at it. Consistency is key. Building a tribe takes time and effort. Stay patient and persistent, and over time, you can create a thriving community of like-minded individuals who share your passions and goals.

How to Disagree with Bosses and Colleagues

When you are younger, you are likely to not want to express your true opinions at the workplace. You may not agree with an idea being discussed for a client. You may think the strategy of the company is wrong. You may have another suggestion for how things should be done. You may not like the way a colleague has been treated. These are all opportunities to express your opinion.

But something holds you back. Maybe you had a bad experience of being shut down when you expressed yourself. Maybe you worry about the consequences of having a view contrary to what the CEO thinks. Maybe you don't want to risk being seen as the one who constantly raises red flags and questions authority.

Do you remain silent and unnoticed?

I believe you will start losing your professional integrity and responsibility to yourself if you don't contribute with your opinion. I am not saying you should be opinionated and have an opposing view on everything. Don't make that your identity either. But you should choose to be the kind of professional who does not take things at face value. Think deeply, contribute consciously and don't be afraid. Yes, in some work environments, it may be the kiss of death to speak up but even in those situations, there are ways to make yourself heard. Even if you are not listened to, at least you have done your part of sharing your views.

My strategy is to wait patiently for the right moment to interject with my opinion. I start by asking for permission to offer a different perspective. This will ensure that people sit up and pay attention. It will also state the intent that it is just about considering another perspective. I won't speak up until that permission has been given.

I speak in a calm, confident, self-assured and respectful manner. I won't attack the senior person upfront saying that I disagree. I reinforce that it is just my perspective, not necessarily the right one. I may choose to ask a clarifying question to deepen my understanding. I may suggest an alternative way of looking at the situation. I may offer different solutions. I may outline the impact of a chosen strategy that others may not have thought of.

Whatever the circumstance, I position my point of view as a consideration of what is right for the business. I never make it personal or emotional. I don't get flustered if I am shut down immediately or if people don't like what I am saying. I don't see it as a personal failure if my point doesn't prevail. I express myself and keep the conversation open and positive. And then I move on.

It may be hard to do the first time, but it gets easier with practice. You have to keep reminding yourself to not make it personal.

How to Ask for Anything

If you don't ask, you don't get. But what do you do if you are terrible at asking for what you want? *Hard Asks Made Easy* by Laura Fredricks will give you practical, actionable tips on how to get exactly what you want by asking the right questions. From Laura, I learned five principles of asking which may help you too.

Principle 1
Frame what you want in very specific terms. What do you want by when? Specificity narrows the scope of objections, and a time-bound request is more likely to improve the responsiveness even if there are objections you can talk through. Think of the difference between these two questions: Shall we go out of town for a quick break next weekend? Can we decide by the end of the day tomorrow whether we will go to X, Y or Z for a quick break?

Principle 2
Write down at least fifteen objections that you may encounter and how you will respond to each. Using the example above, you might get the following challenges: I have to work again, I can't go. It's too expensive, let's not spend money. I'm not in a mood. We can't leave the dogs alone. And so on. What Laura teaches is to think through your response to each objection that could come up. Be creative and think hard of all the possible objections. Fifteen is given as the number of objections to aim for so that you can go deeper than just thinking through the obvious ones. This level of preparation improves your odds of getting to a yes faster.

Principle 3
Deliver your ask with supreme confidence. It should not be a weak request. Put your passion into it. Your presence should exude your desire. Turn off distractions so you are fully present in the moment you're asking for what you want. You may want to stand when you ask, if appropriate.

Principle 4

Inevitably, you will receive objections. You are seldom going to get a yes straightaway. If that were the case, you would have not been hesitant to ask in the first place. Once you listen to the objections, play back what you heard. Make the other person feel fully heard and understood. Then you can take on each objection with your carefully thought out responses.

Principle 5

Plan your response on the go. You may encounter objections you had not anticipated. Thinking on your feet will be required here. The prep you had done with the fifteen questions you had anticipated is bound to help you get through unanticipated objections better. Every time we ask an important question, we can make it a conversation and an opportunity to deepen your relationship with the other person.

How to Overcome Limiting self-Beliefs

AP Dhillon, an Indo-Canadian singer, rapper and record producer, has a brand of unwavering self-belief. Record labels rejected his music because they couldn't understand it. It didn't neatly fit into any category. But he had unlimited love and passion for the music that he was making and enjoyed it so much that he persisted with producing the music he loved. Ultimately, with his band he created songs that exploded in popularity on YouTube which then led to concerts and that's how his fame spread. Social media had a big role to play in this. That's an oversimplification of AP's story, but it does highlight the importance of self-belief against all odds which is not atypical to the journeys of striving artists. To be clear, self-belief wasn't the only factor that led to his huge success, but it was a big element.

I mentor many young men and women who are in their early and mid-careers. I am also a mother to two teenage daughters. This gives me a lot of exposure to how young people view themselves and their talents. The pattern that I see is self-sabotage because of limiting self-beliefs.

If you believe you can't, you won't. If you believe you can, you will.

Why is it that every individual does not have unshakeable confidence in their own abilities?

Childhood experiences play a part. You may have been labelled as an unathletic child when growing up. You were just never able to shake off this label. It may have impacted you so much that you subconsciously shunned exercise for the rest of your life.

Fear of failure plays a part. You may be weighed down by the expectations that your family and friends have of you. That fear eats into your self-confidence and paralyses you.

A lack of self-worth contributes to this as well. This is intimately tied to self-belief. You may not value yourself because you never truly felt valued for who you are and what your inherent talents are. You were always trying to be somebody others wanted you to be. This diminishes your self-worth while adversely impacting your self-belief.

Often, when I am guiding someone on personal branding, it becomes a futile exercise. This is because they are trying to package something that is weak on the inside. You cannot have a strong personal brand if you don't believe in yourself. So that is where you must start.

What might be some ways in which you can overcome limiting self-beliefs? Are there things you can do before you seek help from a professional?

Here are all the things you should try to overcome your limiting self-belief.

Identify and acknowledge

Start by looking inside. Spend time with yourself to understand what is holding you back from reaching your full potential. What negative beliefs do you have about your capabilities? Where have they come from?

Challenge

Question these thoughts. Are they valid? Or are they just playing up in your mind as a reaction to things people may have told you?

Reframe

Try to reframe what you think. Perhaps you think you are a terrible strategist. Reframe it to tell yourself there are tasks in strategy that you love and those that you don't. You are a hardworking strategist who finds ease with some parts of the job but must put in much more effort into others. Labelling yourself as a terrible strategist is limiting your outlook.

Collect evidence

When you look at things more calmly, is there evidence to challenge your self-limiting beliefs? Maybe you think you are not a runner, but you can recall how you sprinted almost a kilometre to make your flight in time. It is proof that you can move!

Set practical goals

Instead of thinking you are fat and have to lose 20 kgs, break that down into what you might have to do every day to achieve that goal. Perhaps it starts with just a little effort every day toward becoming the healthy person you wish to be.

Visualise success

Vision boards are all the rage and they do work. When you can dream it, you know you can do it. Conjure up vividly what success looks like. Use photos, key words, whatever it takes to inspire and motivate you to reach your goals.

Be kind to yourself

Overcoming your self-beliefs won't be a journey that happens at the snap of your fingers. It's a journey of persistence and perseverance. You will veer off the path many times. Be kind to yourself. Acknowledge it is part of the journey and keep moving forward.

Get support

It does not have to be a lonely journey. Share your struggles with your family and friends. They can be a great encouragement.

Keep growing
Invest in up-skilling. Take some classes. Watch some videos. Learning gives you the positive boost you need.

Practise positive affirmation
While this sounds hokey, and I have struggled with putting positive affirmations to practice, it has worked for me. I am on a journey of health and wellness, but there are days on which I fall off the wagon. I must keep reminding myself (despite the junk I have indulged in!) that I am a healthy and fit person who does right by her body every day. This positive affirmation quickly snaps me back on track.

Journal
It's a good idea to document your journey in a journal. It helps to go back and understand yourself and your actions better.

How to Handle Rejection

Rejection can be hugely damaging to the psyche.

You don't get promoted at work. What do you conclude? That you're not as smart as your co-workers or that your boss doesn't like you.

Your child doesn't get selected for the school play. She gets into a tailspin on how she doesn't have any talent. You start to think maybe it's you. You perhaps gave her poor genes!

A cherished relationship breaks-up. You think you're a loser. Nobody loves you.

You don't hear back after a first date. You conclude you're not as hot/handsome/pretty as you thought you were.

You send a pitch about your first book to many publishers. Nobody calls back. You think you're a lousy writer who is never going to get published.

We've all experienced rejection, big and small, in our lives. It can be piercing with the pain lingering for days, sometimes months or even years.

I used to have a maths tutor in high school who never got over the pain of having been rejected by his first lover. He swore never to like women again. He subconsciously carried around this negativity for the rest of his life. I still remember feeling his bitterness every time I met him even though I was so removed from his life story.

In my own career, I was booted off a prestigious project when I worked at Landor's London office. The pain of that rejection lasted for months. Even now (more than fifteen years later) when I think about it, there is a teeny-weeny remnant of hurt. Maybe I was just not good enough.

Rejection can be hugely damaging to the psyche. If we let it.

Is there a way to put it aside and get on with life?

The number one mistake we make is that we allow rejection to impact our identity and self-worth.

Not getting a promotion does not mean you are not smart.

Your child not getting selected for one school play doesn't mean she is not talented.

A break-up doesn't mean you are a loser.

A rejection after a first date doesn't mean you don't have good looks or a desirable personality.

Not getting called by a publisher doesn't mean you are not a good writer.

All it means is that in that instance, you were not chosen.

There could have been numerous reasons as to why you were rejected that have nothing to do with you.

Even if it had to do with you, you shouldn't make this an indictment on yourself that could possibly take years to recover from.

Deal with the rejection. Sleep over it. Brood all you want for twenty-four hours. Then, let it go. Don't connect it to your sense of self-worth and identity. It's best to work with a therapist who can unpack this for you.

What you can do though is to think about what the rejection has taught you. Where could you have done things differently? Can you improve in one way or another? What is this rejection telling you that could be useful to your life.

I love how Sylvester Stallone thinks about rejection. 'I take rejection as someone blowing a bugle in my ear to wake me up and get going, rather than retreat.'

This is a very powerful and practical way to cope with rejection – to just get on with it.

How to Overcome Internal Barriers to Success

'Most barriers to your success are man-made. And most often, you're the man who made them,' says Frank Tyger.

There isn't much written or talked about internal barriers to success at the workplace, especially for women. We have so many talented and ambitious women entering the workplace every year but only a fraction of these women make it to senior levels.

External barriers like the culture of the organisation, gender bias, lack of flexibility, pay gap and other elements are not in our control. While these factors certainly hinder the ability of many women to succeed, the key to unlocking opportunity for women is to simultaneously overcome internal barriers that are holding us back. These include self-limiting beliefs, lack of confidence, staying in our comfort zones, and not tapping into others for help.

Self-limiting Beliefs

The problem is this: For generations, societal conditioning has laid out how men and women should act. From a very young age, many girls are repeatedly told that they are not strong enough or smart enough and that they are not as important as boys. Their personas are cultivated to be respectful, polite and helpful to others. As a result, when many women enter the workplace, they bring with them an inner voice that continually doubts their own competence and worth. This results in a lack of faith in what they can accomplish, even though they may have the brightest mind or highest potential among their peer group.

Silencing the inner critic is critical for a woman's career progression and vital for her to thrive in senior positions.

Here are three ways to silence your inner critic:

Practice self-compassion

Cultivate self-compassion by treating yourself with the same kindness and understanding that you would offer to a close friend. When your inner critic starts to berate you, counteract those negative thoughts with positive and compassionate self-talk. Remind yourself that everyone makes mistakes, has flaws and goes through difficult times. Be understanding and forgiving towards yourself. Mindfulness and meditation techniques can also help you become more aware of your thoughts and feelings, making it easier to respond to self-critical thoughts with self-compassion.

Challenge negative thoughts
Actively challenge your negative thoughts. When you catch yourself being self-critical, question the validity of these thoughts. Ask yourself if there is any evidence to support these negative beliefs. Often, you'll realise that your inner critic is exaggerating or distorting the truth. Replace these negative thoughts with positive affirmations or statements that are based on evidence and reality. For instance, if your inner critic says, 'I'm terrible at everything,' counteract it with evidence of your past successes or compliments you've received from others. Cognitive behavioural therapy (CBT) techniques can be particularly helpful in identifying and challenging negative thought patterns.

Develop a growth mindset
Cultivate a growth mindset, which is the belief that your abilities and intelligence can be developed with effort, learning and dedication. Embrace challenges and view failures as opportunities to learn and grow rather than as indications of your worth. When your inner critic tells you that you're not good enough, remind yourself that you are a work in progress and that making mistakes is a natural part of the learning process. Celebrate your efforts and progress, no matter how small they may seem. By adopting a growth mindset, you can change the way you perceive yourself and your abilities, leading to a positive self-image.

Lack of Confidence

Imposter syndrome – the feeling that you don't deserve your job and are an imposter who can be found out at any moment – is a feeling familiar to many women. In fact, an academic study found that this syndrome affects close to 70 per cent of people at some point, prominently women. Imposter syndrome means that while we may be accomplished, we still don't rate ourselves as highly as our male counterparts. We don't speak up and let our voice be heard. We are not aggressive in asking for more. We worry disproportionately about not being liked, outshining others or promoting ourselves too much. A study from Cornell University found that men overestimate their abilities and performance, while women underestimate both. In reality, women's actual performances do not differ in quality or quantity from men's on average. And yet the confidence difference based in gender is real. For women who want to succeed in today's world, believing that you can accomplish anything is a critical starting point. Innovative training programs that bring women together and help them build self-confidence can go a long way in shaping the women leaders of tomorrow.

Here are three ways to overcome imposter syndrome:

Acknowledge and reframe your thoughts

Recognise that imposter syndrome is a common feeling that many successful individuals experience. When you catch yourself thinking that you don't deserve your accomplishments, consciously challenge these thoughts. Reframe negative self-talk into positive affirmations. Focus on your skills, experiences and the hard work that led you to where you are. Remind yourself that your achievements are a result of your abilities and efforts.

Celebrate your achievements

Take time to acknowledge and celebrate your successes, no matter how small they might seem. Keep a journal of your accomplishments, skills and positive feedback from others. Whenever you feel like an imposter, revisit this journal to reinforce your self-confidence. Celebrating your achievements can help you internalise your successes and counteract feelings of inadequacy.

Seek support and mentorship

Connect with a supportive network of friends, family or colleagues who can provide encouragement and perspective. Share your feelings of self-doubt with trusted individuals, as they can offer reassurance and help you gain a more realistic view of your abilities. Additionally, consider finding a mentor, especially a successful woman in your field, who can offer guidance, share their own experiences with imposter syndrome and provide valuable advice on how to navigate these feelings.

Staying in the Comfort Zone

Perhaps one of the most limiting career moves women fall prey to is staying in our comfort zones. As we get older and more comfortable with our jobs, it can seem easier to go with the flow rather than doing something to shake up the status quo. It's scary to step out and try something challenging—something you never thought possible. Fear of the unknown, fear of failure and fear of judgement often hold us back. But it is this very leap that women need to make in order to grow and progress. We must keep picking up new skills. We must be the first to raise our hands when opportunities come along and the first to confidently take the plunge into the unknown when the time is right. Once we trust ourselves to do this, the confidence gained from stepping out of our comfort zone directly impacts our self-esteem and outlook on life.

Not Tapping into Others

You have to be strategic about who you choose as a mentor because of the power that others can have in your career. Women should look at their own industry – and even outside it – to make a list of the top people who can really help them achieve their ambitions. It's then up to each of us to make these connections or find ways to be introduced to our top influencers in real life. In some cases, it may take a while to reach the top people you want to meet, but it never hurts to ask – and you'll be surprised how often it's a 'yes' rather than a 'no.' Outside of merely building our own networks, women should be mentors to others. By opening up our networks and sharing contacts and resources generously, we deliberately treat others as we hope we'll be treated in return.

Reaching the Finish Line

While there are still many external barriers that we may not have direct control over, internal barriers to success are elements that we can work to overcome. To succeed, women will have to spend time reflecting and focusing on themselves, pushing themselves to step outside their comfort zones and take on new challenges with confidence. Coupled with a supportive and encouraging work environment, we can take ourselves – and the women around us – further than we ever dreamed possible.

Conclusion

'The woods are lovely dark and deep,
But I have promises to keep,
And miles to go before I sleep,
And miles to go before I sleep.'

These memorable lines from 'Stopping by Woods on a Snowy Evening' by Robert Frost were taught to me in the seventh grade. While I didn't initially grasp the true meaning of what Frost was conveying through the poem, the lines come back to me and resonate strongly even to this day.

I believe immensely in the emerging concept of the 100-Year Life. Research has shown how human life expectancy has increased significantly in the past few decades and how many of us are expected to live well into our nineties, if not likely to hit the century mark. This means that our life's work is not done when we expect it to. Rather, we should aim to do a lot more before we can finally rest.

I am around the mid-century point now though I haven't yet reached my fiftieth birthday. I have spent a quarter of a century getting ready for work. I have spent another quarter dedicating myself to work. I have a quarter more to go in my career. And then the last quarter will be active retirement. That is the way I'm looking at how my 100-Year Life will stack up.

The process of writing this book has been wonderfully rewarding, because in sharing my learnings, I could reminisce many of my life experiences. I found myself taking writer Anne Lamott's advice of forensically excavating my childhood and teenage years for stories. The vignettes that I pulled together and articulated for this book have given me a deeper appreciation of my journey because of the vantage point and the benefit of hindsight.

While I am proud of my career accomplishments up to the present, I do have a long way to go to contribute more and leave behind a richer professional and personal legacy.

What might I have done differently in the first twenty-five years of my career? What will I do differently in the next twenty-five?

There are three things I would tell my younger self.

Never stop learning

When I look back on all the free time I had before kids and before my work responsibilities became significant, I regret having whiled away time on leisure pursuits like eating out, partying, watching movies and 'chilling out' – these are surely important elements of having a good life, but they should not be the only things on the agenda when you are starting your career. It can't just be work hard and play hard. That becomes a rather hedonistic and unidimensional lifestyle which I regret having vigorously pursued in my early years.

I wish I had understood the importance of always learning new things even after I graduated from business school and had started working. I now understand the importance of creating a learning syllabus every year and dedicating time every day to learning. This applies not only to hard technical skills relevant to my job but also soft skills like empathy, emotional intelligence and negotiation as well as hobbies and creative pursuits.

I didn't reflect much or have a practice of journaling in the early years. This could have made such a huge difference to quickly adapting my style and evolving as a professional based on the mistakes being made.

I also wish I had found mentors early on. I could have learned so much from their experience. Who knows, my career might have been accelerated even earlier!

Never stop having fun!

This second point may be contradictory to what I said in the previous paragraph, but it's not. So many times, in my career, I gave my all to work, leaving no time for anything else. As I grew more senior in the organisation, this became more acute. I had a mistaken view of how irreplaceable I was and an exaggerated view of my own importance. So, I was thinking of work 24/7. Many times, even when on holiday I was switched on to the office via the laptop and mobile phone. I missed friends' birthdays, family events and some of my daughters' school milestones because I was at work.

I was taking myself too seriously and giving work way more importance than it deserved. It wasn't as though anyone was forcing me to work all the time. It wasn't company policy either. I just didn't know better. I had sucked all the fun out of my life and had become the workaholic I never wanted to be.

It wasn't until a close friend gave me a dressing-down and made me realise there was more to life than just work that I started making time for more fun activities.

Fun can be whatever floats your boat. A day spent at the spa or out at the beach with friends, a movie night, a blow-out party, comedy shows on YouTube or even digital detox. It has to be moments when you switch off work totally and immerse yourself in something that will relax you, make you laugh and allow you to shake off all the stress that inevitably accumulates from a high-pressure job.

I also resisted quick weekend getaway trips and a lot of travel because I didn't want to miss out on work. Again, I wish I could turn back the clock on all those lost experiences. Travel is so enriching. It can greatly enhance creativity. I realised this only years later.

Never stop protecting your wellbeing

It is only now I realise the critical importance of health and overall well-being. The trigger was when my mother was diagnosed with breast cancer the first time around. It shook me out of my ignorance. I had read Vijay Bhatt's *My Cancer is Me*, which made me realise the emotional and the environmental triggers for the growth of cancer cells. I had to do a better job of protecting my health.

When I was young I thought I was invincible. I would boast about how little sleep I needed. I prided myself on being able to pull all-nighters. It was thrilling to lead a hectic work life full of travel from one exciting city to the next. There was no time for rest and relaxation. How wrong I was!

After the birth of my first daughter, I went back to work after two months. After the birth of my second, it was around the same duration of maternity leave. When I look back now, both were too soon. I envy my colleagues giving birth today and if they live in a country with progressive maternity policies, they may even take a whole year off. I wish I had the option to take a year off each time. It would have surely deepened the bonding experience with my daughters.

I also didn't pay much attention to the rising trend of meditation a few decades ago when it was not mainstream. I thought it was an activity suited for the retired, not one for busy individuals. Given what I now know about the transformative benefits of meditation, I would have started a meditation practice much earlier, maybe even as early as in high school.

Similarly, I wasn't aware of my poor posture and my frequent yawning. The former was because nobody had bothered to correct me and the latter because I wasn't breathing properly. These seem like small things, but the right approach on both fronts early on would have been very beneficial.

And then of course there is eating healthy food and exercising regularly. Both take a huge hit when you travel frequently. It becomes difficult to be consistent. It requires the right mindset and fastidious planning, both of which I lacked when I was younger.

So if these are the three things I would tell my younger self, what would I tell my older self?

Listen more

I've progressed as a listener, but I still have miles to go.

If I could shut out distractions and be fully present, it would vastly improve how those with whom I have close relationships feel about me. They love me and accept me the way I am but deep inside I sense I disappoint them. The acceptance is something that is grudgingly cloaked in 'I know how busy you are'. I am filled with guilt when I hear such statements. My 'busyness' should never be an excuse.

I want to listen more to seniors. They have the most fascinating stories and life adventures to share. I need to make more time for that.

I want to listen more to youngsters. Their unjaded world view and fresh perspectives are so energising.

I want to listen more to sounds of the natural world. There is so much peace, joy and wisdom to be found in the outdoors if I could only harness it more often.

And I want to listen more to myself, which means practicing a lot more silence to connect deeply with myself.

Give more

I've progressed as a giver and not just a taker, but I still have a long way to go!

As I get older, I want to give more and hoard less – both physically and metaphorically.

I want to give more time, more energy, more attention and more money away.

In each of these areas I want to give more both professionally and personally. More active involvement in mentoring and sponsorship of women, more positions on advisory boards of non-profits and more philanthropy are some of the areas I want to double down on in my third quarter.

I passionately believe that I came to the world having nothing. I must leave this world with nothing as well other than a legacy which lives on in the hearts and souls of the people whose lives I was able to impact in some way.

Die Empty is a book by Todd Henry which cautions you not to go to the grave with your ideas buried with you. It's an urgent call to action to pour it all out. I interpret it as giving it all away. Seizing each day and giving it your best so there are no regrets no matter when it is time for you to leave.

Risk more

I've progressed in taking more calculated risks in different areas of my life, but I still have miles to go! I rate myself quite conservatively in my decisions and actions. I'm a little tired of having played it safe. 'No risk, no reward' is something that haunts me from time to time. I've lived quite a safe life thus far. The third quarter of my life is going to be about more risk.

I want to push myself much harder and I'm not going to be afraid of failure. I want to explore what's next – maybe a different second career, maybe an entrepreneurial venture, maybe a TV show, maybe a change of country. The list is endless. The possibilities are super exciting. I'm going to become more courageous and welcome them with wider arms than ever before!

Author Elizabeth Gilbert's wise words from *Big Magic* are my compass: 'The treasures that are hiding inside you are hoping you will say yes.'

Writing this book has given me so much energy to listen more, give more and risk more in my life.

I hope that you've enjoyed the stories based on my journey and that there are ideas in here that you can apply to your career to go further, faster!

I look forward to continuing the conversation with you online; you can find me on my personal wesbite (luluraghavan.com), LinkedIn or Instagram.

See you there!

Acknowledgements

THE IDEA FOR A book came from several friends who have observed my journey over the last few decades. 'You should write a book, Lulu', was something I heard very often but didn't act on.

This book was born from a conversation I had with Landor London's design director Pavithra Dikshit, who is also my cover designer. She said if not now it will be too late and I had to just do it! Thank you, Pavi, for that kick at just the right time, and for your vibrant cover design. I am grateful for all the time you have given to this passion project of mine.

It was Pavithra who led me to Chinmayee Manjunath, my writing coach, who has been there every step of the way from the moment I conceptualised the structure for the book and pitched it to her to the completion of my manuscript. Chinmayee introduced me to the world of publishing and was a patient companion throughout. Her encouragement was a huge contributor to getting my book done. Our regular check-ins helped me stay on track and her feedback was instrumental in honing in on my unique voice.

To R. Gopalakrishnan, or Gopal Chittappa as I call him, thank you so much for believing in me, supporting me and for facilitating an introduction to Bloomsbury.

To Krishan, Paul, Meenakshi, Krittika and the entire team at Bloomsbury, thank you so much for your enthusiasm for the book from the get-go and your support throughout.

I am very grateful to P.V. Sindhu for the foreword. When I reached out to her and explained what the book is about and who it is meant for, she agreed right away. She has achieved success and global recognition through ambition, determination and immense hard work. There is so much we can all learn from her journey.

I am also super grateful to all the senior leaders who extended their support: Leena Nair, Shantanu Narayen, Angela Arhendts,

Jane Geraghty, Falguni Nayar, Anand Mahindra, Harish Bhat, Pooja Dhingra, Dr Ranjan Banerjee, Julia Middleton, Tanya Dubash and Debbie Millman.

A very special thanks to my dear clients and colleagues at Landor and friends who contributed mini essays to my book sharing their experiences with my readers: Asha Kharga, Madhuri Ruia, Jyotika Purwar, Pavithra Dikshit, Dr Cecilia Chettiar, Komal Rajani, Louise Corbett and Ronita Mukerjee.

While the common adage is that there is a woman behind every man's success, the reverse is also true. I've had several men who have been huge pillars of strength in different ways. Big thanks to my dad, my husband and my former colleague Manil Dodani, all of whom have supported me in more ways than I ever imagined. And to each of the ten male bosses I have had in my 23-year career at Landor. Each one of them has made me a better person and given me opportunities to shine brightly. A special thanks to Jonathan Cummings, my current boss who is the President of APAC at Landor. His belief in my abilities and the opportunities he has given me have helped me get to the next level in my career. I feel truly lucky to work at an organisation like Landor and passionately believe that so many colleagues over my almost 24 years at the company have contributed to my success.

A huge shout-out to my family (especially my in-laws who have always supported and cheered me), friends and everyone on social media who has been super enthusiastic and excited about the book ever since I announced I was writing one. Your anticipation was my motivation!

The last acknowledgement is for my mother who told me more than a decade ago that I should write a book on 'celebritising' yourself. I didn't know what she meant but I'm certain that the idea that she seeded in me is what finally germinated, sprouted and flourished into the book you are holding in your hands. Hence, I've dedicated all the royalty I earn from this book to her non-profit organisation, Dignity Foundation, of which I am a trustee.

Thank you, dear reader, for giving your time and attention to this book. Feel free to reach out to me on email: lulu.raghavan@gmail.com. I hope you are walking away with at least a few ideas that can be transformative in your life and with which you can indeed go further, faster.

About My Professional Journey

I AM PASSIONATE ABOUT HELPING young women prepare for the future of work. I didn't realise the importance of preparation until much later in life when a former boss often repeated a quote attributed to the Roman philosopher Seneca: 'Luck is what happens when preparation meets opportunity.' He used to say this in the context of winning new business pitches, but I took a broader view of its meaning. Had I been better prepared with the right mindset and a library of tools for advancement, I might have seized big career opportunities earlier in my life. I want to pass on this message to young women who have entered the corporate world with big dreams in their hearts.

I have a very vivid memory of when my joy for teaching and helping others first captured my imagination. At the age of four, growing up in Indiranagar in Bangalore, my favourite game to play was to sit in my sprawling lush garden with a blackboard and a ruler teaching my dogs Waddle and Sasha everything from English to Maths. My canine friends encouraged me by giving me their rapt attention.

My love for expressing myself through writing was seeded when my first published piece on The Neem Tree appeared in The Valley School's yearly publication when I was in class four. In class seven, I won a national competition when I penned an article on the importance of the girl child.

In addition to reading and writing, I was very sporty as a young girl. I won scores of school medals in athletics, swimming, badminton, basketball, table tennis and cross-country to name a few sports I excelled in. All this was over and above my academic excellence leading to being named Queen Mary School's Rotary International Awardee for 'Best All-Rounder of the Year' in class ten. I continued collecting accolades in High School, and then graduated from Cathedral and John Connon having served the school as School Prefect, House Vice-Captain, Badminton Captain, and Basketball Captain.

While in high school, my mother encouraged me to apply to colleges in the US. Despite being an only child from a conservative Tamilian family, I was given the opportunity by my parents to do my undergraduate studies in America. I won a full scholarship to Davidson College in North Carolina. At Davidson, I was the president of the International Students Association and graduated cum laude with a major in Economics and a minor in Applied Mathematics. I was fortunate to spend six months living and studying in France on the 'Davidson in Tours' Study Abroad programme which was a transformative student experience for me as it involved living with a French family, meeting students my age from so many different countries in the world, traveling all over France and only speaking in French and no other language.

I returned to India after my undergrad in the US. I was looking for a job in management consulting or investment banking, two of the most common career choices for Economics graduates. The course of my life after a chance meeting with Sumit Roy, a veteran of the advertising industry. He asked me if I wanted to be 'a small fish in a big pond' or 'a big fish in a small pond'! He went on to help me get a job under the tutelage of R. Sridhar at Ogilvy Brand Consulting. What a dream start to my career at the much-celebrated global advertising agency network Ogilvy & Mather.

I spent a year soaking up all things branding and advertising at Ogilvy. From Sridhar, I picked up a love for business books of which he had an enviable collection. I also learned branding basics while being Sridhar's assistant on consulting projects. It was the first time that an ad agency was trying the consulting model. It was such an honour to be part of this experiment.

During my year at Ogilvy, Sridhar advised me to get an MBA. He couldn't emphasise enough that an undergraduate degree was insufficient to create an impact in the corporate world in India. Heeding his advice, I went on to business school, completing my MBA in International Business and Marketing from S.P. Jain Institute of Management and Research in Mumbai.

By the time I graduated from SPJIMR, I knew that brands were my thing. My love for brands had been born at Ogilvy and nurtured at business school through the case studies, class discussions, course work and the capstone project which I completed on the importance of branding for Indian IT companies to rise up the value chain. After graduation, I briefly worked as the brand manager of AutomartIndia.com (a Mahindra Group venture) before getting married, moving to the US and starting at Landor Associates in San Francisco.

I had been made an offer to join Landor as a naming manager at a time when the business was flourishing. By the time my H1 visa was processed almost six months later, it was a different picture entirely. The dotcom boom had gone bust in Silicon Valley which had a cascading impact on businesses in the Bay Area and beyond. A few weeks after I had joined Landor, the company had its first ever layoffs which involved letting go of a third of its workforce. Alton Wright, Head of Verbal Branding, who had offered me the job was leaving himself. But he saw my potential and his influence with the management to remove my name from the layoff list was perhaps the main reason I managed to hold on to my job despite being the new kid on the block.

There was no looking back. I spent a good three and half years at the San Francisco office learning all aspects of naming and brand strategy. I even got a stint for a year and a half with the then CEO of Landor, Craig Branigan, to be his executive Assistant and corporate strategist. This gave me a solid understanding of the Landor business, our global network, our parent company WPP and importantly, what it would take to succeed.

After a few years, my husband got a job in New York, so we moved there following our time in San Francisco. I was lucky to be accommodated with a transfer to Landor's New York office where I continued to work on naming and brand strategy assignments. It was the best time of my life to be living and working in Manhattan, having a ten-minute walk to our cool office, which was (close to Union Square) understanding impatient and demanding clients and soaking in the vibe of an extremely fast-paced and hectic lifestyle.

Just as I was getting settled in New York, my husband got a transfer to London. I couldn't exactly complain about moving to a glamorous city like London, but what about my job? As luck would have it, Landor was willing to transfer me. There was a position in client servicing that had opened up, so I moved to our London office as a client director. This was an exciting time to be working in the London office. We won a few large assignments for clients in India including Jet Airways. Being part of such a prestigious brand revitalisation programme was the highlight of my career. However, after a few months into the project, I was taken off for reasons that I am still unaware of. That then became a real low and I struggled to find my rhythm in the London office after that.

Luckily, my husband was transferred to India and so I had the good fortune for a fresh start. What an incredible opportunity to finally move back home! We did not have an office in India at that time. We had a few clients like the Taj Group and Hindustan Construction Company (HCC) which we were servicing from our Hong Kong studio. I spoke with our Global CEO and was able to convince him and the leadership team to give me the chance to set up our operations. Charlie Wrench who was our CEO then had a real soft spot for India and believed in its potential as a future market for Landor.

I was paired with Bengt Eriksson, who was then the managing director of the Middle East and based in our Dubai studio. Bengt became my boss and mentor who would guide me to establish our India operations. He visited Mumbai every few weeks to help set up our studio in Mumbai. We pitched aggressively and started winning business from a broad range of clients including Cafe Coffee Day, Sterlite Technologies and Mahindra Group.

We set up Landor in Mumbai by renting a few desks at Grey Advertising (also a WPP company), which had a sprawling office in Parel. The building was beautifully designed with glass walls, lots of indoor plants and a stunning central staircase which was a showstopper. The unique design made our office a sought-after filming location for Bollywood 'office scenes' during the weekends. In the first five years of being in the Grey office, we were a small team of just five women. We were affectionately called 'The Ladies of Landor' by Mr. R.K. Krishna Kumar, who was then the vice chairman of Indian Hotels and Tata Global Beverages, two of Landor's clients.

One of my fondest memories of this phase of my career is that I had an opportunity to have my own TV show on Bloomberg

UTV. One of the editors there had seen my interview about Landor on the channel and wanted a show on branding. She called me one day and asked if I'd be interested in doing a TV show. It was the most fun thing I'd done in a while. Having my own show tested a broad range of my skills from conceptual thinking to interviewing to on-screen presence. With the help of my colleagues, we came up with Beyond Logo which was to educate audiences about the power of branding. In each episode, I had twenty-four minutes to interview the CEO of a top company to get them to talk about the value of branding. Beyond Logo put me on the map as a personal brand to be reckoned with both internally across the global network at Landor and with potential employees and clients in India.

As our team grew, we moved to a larger space at Peninsula Centre, also in Parel, where we spent the next three years. Our office was right next to the Mid-Day Radio office, so we often spotted Bollywood stars coming in for on-air interviews. This office could easily accommodate fifteen employees, but we managed to squeeze in twenty-two at one point. We had a small meeting room where all of us would squeeze in for daily meetings. It was also where we hosted our clients. Despite our small size, through the design, we managed to create a warm vibe that was very attractive to current and potential employees.

Our next phase of growth and office space was one of the most memorable. We moved in to share space with Fitch, the retail design agency, also part of WPP. Fitch had a sprawling office on the 20th floor of India Bulls Finance which opened onto an equally large terrace with spectacular views of either side of the bay. On a clear day, on one side we could see the Sea Link and the Bombay Harbour on the other. We had taken the side of the office which flowed onto the terrace where we had lunch every day and hosted much talked about parties. The Landor space had all the vibes of a buzzing creative studio. Every potential employee who walked in commented on the special ambiance. I was happy that at every location we moved to, we managed to create a desirable workspace which I know intuitively was critical for employee engagement.

While we were co-located with Fitch, we didn't interact with the Fitch employees much except by bumping into them in the washrooms we shared. They resented us taking up part of their space and there was some kind of unspoken rivalry. Both sides had their guards up. Somehow, we just couldn't get our friendship going. Who knew we would all end up working for the same company just a few years later and would be forced to merge cultures and work as one unified team!

Before the merger of Landor and Fitch, both agencies had to leave their fantastic office space in India Bulls and take up space at the new WPP Campus in Andheri. Both agencies resisted the move for as long as we could, but it was inevitable. We ended up taking space on the third floor (Landor) and fourth floor (Fitch) of the Mumbai international airport. While we complained bitterly about the move, we quickly found our rhythm at the new campus and enjoyed the space more than we had imagined. We designed an equally stunning Landor office to match the spectacular view of the airport and runway.

As luck would have it, the world got hit by the pandemic. Overnight, we had to pack all our personal belongings, not knowing when we would return to work. As it so happened, it took eighteen months to get back into the WPP Campus. And when we did, we were a new company, Landor & Fitch. Landor decided to give up its space on the third floor. Fitch's space on the fourth floor was renamed 'Landor & Fitch'. We didn't do much by way of an office redress immediately but have gradually been sprucing up the space to make it creatively inspiring.

I was honoured to be made the managing director of the combined entity, Landor & Fitch in India. Overnight, I went from managing a small team to a large one of just under seventy-five employees. While I was elated to have gotten the top job, I knew I had a tough task ahead. Merging the operations of two vastly different cultures was no mean feat. Having to do this during Covid-19 was even harder. I had to lean into all my learnings on leadership and advice from mentors to get it right.

The year that followed was one of the most challenging but also transformative for my career. It was the year in which I finally transitioned from manager to leader. I had to create a common vision, shared values and define a modus operandi for delivering results. I was lucky to have a very ambitious, talented and driven leadership team and a broader workforce that was hungry to do good work. All that was required was to create the conditions for growth through the culture of the combined organisation. This led to extraordinary results in the few years that followed on all the key metrics that Landor & Fitch's market leaders are measured against – culture, client satisfaction, awards and of course, revenue and profit growth.

As a result of India's performance and my growth as a market leader in the Landor & Fitch network, I was promoted to vice president of APAC which includes five key markets: India, China, Japan, Australia and Southeast Asia. APAC is one of three regions in our global network, the other two being the Americas and EMEA (Europe, Middle East and Africa). This involves working closely with our president for the region and with all the market leaders to grow the business in Asia.

My new role has new challenges, the biggest one being working effectively with diverse teams across diverse cultures. This region is among the most culturally diverse in the world.

It's important to understand the cultural context in which employees, clients and consumers operate in order to make the right decisions. The excitement of the role is the opportunity to broaden my sphere of influence as a leader and mentor leaders and their teams to rise to their full potential.

As I'm growing, I'm also shaping my style of leadership to transcend borders and be truly universal. This would prepare me well for the future

Landor & Fitch has now been rebranded to Landor.

Index

4-7-8 breathing, 53
5 AM Club, 29
360 Degree Perception Audit, 116, 118

Active listening, 80, 134, 167, 169, 186
Amazon, 42, 172
Amex Luxury Summit, 23, 25
Andheri 28
Apple, 5–6, 112
Aristotle, 115
Artificial intelligence, 7
Atomic Habits, 33
Authenticity, 72, 92–95, 104, 115, 127

Bangalore, 57, 110
Beauvoir, Simone de, 5
Beckham, David, 111
Beyond Logo, 20
Bezos, Jeff, 43
Bhatt, Vijay, 83, 207
Bickson, Raymond, 23–24
Big hairy audacious goals (BHAGs), 15
Big Magic, 20, 210
Blyton, Enid, 4, 13
Body language, 168, 189
Box breathing, 53
Bragitude, 174
Brand equity, 103, 142, 153
Brand transformation, 14, 23
Brand voice, 103, 133–135, 140
Brand YOU on a page, 137–141
Branson, Richard, 113, 171
Breath: The New Science of a Lost Art, 50
Brown, Brene, 95, 173–174
Buffet, Warren, 7
Bullet journaling, 43

Cameron, Julia, 17
Camus, 5, 18
Cannes, 25–26
Cannes Lions Festival of Creativity, 25
Charlotte, 5–6
Chatterjee. Upamanyu, 5
Chettiar, Dr Cicilia, 10
Chinna Chokkikulam, 4
Churchgate, 28
Circadian rhythm, 27, 54, 63
Clear, James, 10, 33
Consistency, 16, 104–105, 115, 122, 136, 149–152, 193
Corbett, Louise, 73–74, 165
Covid-19, 64, 68, 73–74, 146, 193
COVID-19 pandemic, 8, 54, 87, 146
Cruisers, The, 1–2

Davidson College, 5, 17, 43, 48–49, 92
Delhi, 54, 57
Design thinking, 76, 101, 123
Digital transformation, 7
Disruption, 6
Divyaprabhandam, 27
Diwekar, Rutuja, 59
Doordarshan, 4

Double Diamond Design Thinking Model, 101

Eat That Frog, 14
Eisenhower Matrix, 43
Emotional intelligence (EI), 11, 72, 78–82, 95, 169, 206
Empathy, 7, 20, 45, 47, 72, 76–78, 80, 95, 127, 133, 167, 169, 175, 206
Energy drainers, 54, 56
Energy givers, 54, 56
English August, 5
Epstein, David, 44

Ferrazzi, Keith, 86, 147
Five-whys technique, 123
Fredricks, Laura, 195
France, 13, 25, 61
Frankl, Victor, 75
Freudenfreude, 173–174

Generalist, 43–45
Geraghty, Jane, 33
Gilbert, Elizabeth, 20, 210
Glassdoor, 185, 188
Google, 25, 132
Gratitude journaling, 59, 80
Gulmarg, 54, 57

Habit stacking, 10
Half a Life, 5
Handwriting as an enhancer of one's identity, 17
Hardy, Benjamin, 14
Henry, Todd, 34, 110, 132, 160–161, 209
Hong Kong, 73
Huffington, Arianna, 57, 171
Humbition, 162–163
Hyderabad, 24, 57–58

Ignite, 25–26
Imposter syndrome, 202–203
Inchauspé, Jessie, 62
Inclusivity, 134
Instagram, 32, 40, 56, 62, 86, 88, 108, 144–145, 151, 164, 193, 210
Intermittent fasting, 63–64
Interoception, 11–12

Jobs, Steve,
  and connecting the dots, 34, 36
  and Sculley, John, 5
Johari Window, 117–118, 120–121, 126, 138
Journaling, 12–17, 35, 80, 84, 115, 199, 206

Kapalabhati, 53
Keller, Gary, 42
Kierkegaard, 5

Lahiri, Jhumpa, 5
Leadership, 14, 18, 31, 36, 40, 45, 72, 94, 133, 145–147, 152, 163, 165, 175–177, 179
leap.club, 35, 178–179
Lee, Ingrid Fettel, 87–88
Lew, Claire, 46
LinkedIn, 21, 40, 56, 85–86, 108, 131, 135, 144–146, 150–151, 153, 162, 164, 188, 210
London, 23, 37–38, 56, 79, 92, 110, 199
Lovecat, 72, 96–98

Madurai, 4
Man's Search for Meaning, 75
Management, 3, 14, 21, 26–29, 31–32, 37, 43, 45, 47, 53–54, 65, 70, 84, 92, 103, 175, 181
Meditation, 10, 12–13, 29–30, 35, 84, 115–116, 201, 208
Mehta, Sanjeev, 113, 162
Meta (formerly Facebook), 25, 108, 193

Metaskills: The Five Talents for the Future of Work, 21
Meta skill, 21
Mind–Body–Soul approach, 2
Mind enrichment, 29–30
Mind management, 3, 26
Mindfulness, 10, 51, 53, 201
Miserables, The, 1–2
Misra, Ajoy, 23–24
Morning Pages, 17
Movement, 29–30, 49, 64–67, 69–70 192
Mukerjee, Ronita, 146
Mumbai (*also* Bombay), 5–6, 8, 23, 28, 61, 72, 92, 128, 193
My Cancer Is Me, 83, 207

Nadi shodhana, 53
Naipaul, V.S., 5
Negotiation, 169, 187, 206
Nestor, James, 50
Neumeier, Marty, 21, 125
Never Eat Alone, 86, 147
Newark, 23
New York, 37, 128
New York Times, 44, 124
Nooyi, Indra, 3–4, 113
North Carolina, 5

Odyssey: Pepsi to Apple, 5
Ogilvy & Mather Advertising, 6
Ogilvy Consulting, 6, 92
Ogilvy, David, 6
Onlyness, 125
See also positioning

Papasan, Jay, 42
PepsiCo, 4
Personal brand guidelines, 137
Personal branding, 35, 101, 104–109, 114–116, 118, 124, 145, 155, 197
Peters, Tom, 104–105
Park City, 23–25
Personality Isn't Permanent, 14
Positioning, 122, 124–126, 128, 139, 143, 150
Positive affirmation, 199, 202–203
Praise-to-criticism ratio, 46
Psychological richness, 88–91

Radical Candor, 47
Range, 44
Redwood City, 28, 67, 160
Resilience, 3, 37, 39, 95, 183
Robbins, Tony, 41
Ruia, Madhuri, 62, 69

San Francisco, 6, 18, 28, 37–38, 66, 92, 179
San Jose, 28
Sanders, Tim, 96–98
Sartre, 5, 18
Scott, Kim, 47
Screwvala, Ronnie, 25
Sculley, John, 5
Self-awareness, 3, 9, 11–13, 72, 79, 84, 91, 93, 117, 121, 175
Self-belief, 26, 186, 196–198
Self-compassion, 174, 201
Self-reflection, 12, 115
See Self-awareness
Sharma, Robin, 29, 55
Shoy, 174
Silence (as a practice), 3, 8–10, 35, 77, 84, 168, 209
Silicon Valley, 28, 164
SP Jain Institute of Management and Research (SPJIMR), 28, 44, 92
Specialist, 43–45

Task management, 43
TBWA, 6
The Accidental Creative, 34
The Confessions of an Advertising Man, 6

The Elements of Style, 18
The One Thing, 42
The Ripple Effect, 49
The Sleep Revolution: Transforming Your Life, One Night at a Time, 57
Thrive: The Third Metric to Redefining Success and Creating a Life of Well-Being, Wisdom, and Wonder, 57
Trudeau, Justin, 111–112
Time blocking, 30–31
Time Management, 3, 26–29, 31–32, 53–54
Tracy, Brian, 14
Twain, Mark, 14

Unaccustomed Strangers, 5
UNICEF, 111
Unilever, 25, 76, 122, 127, 162
USA (*also* the US), 5–6, 13, 22–23, 27, 43, 48–49, 143, 192
Utah, 23

Vision boards, 40, 198
Vishnusahasranamam, 22, 27–28
Visual brand driver, 128, 139
Vulnerability, 36, 72, 92, 94–96

Weil, Dr Andrew, 53
Well, Greg, 49
WhatsApp, 192–193
Whyte, David, 83
Winfrey, Oprah, 112, 136, 171
Women and the Weight Loss Tamasha, 59
Workaholics, The, 1–2, 8
WPP, 25–26, 180
WPP Stella India, 180

X (formerly Twitter), 144–145

YouTube, 68, 144–145, 196, 207

About the Author

Lulu Raghavan, Vice President for Asia Pacific and Managing Director for India at Landor, has spent over two decades with the firm in San Francisco, New York, London and Mumbai and is part of the Global Leadership Team. She spearheaded Landor's growth in India and has led branding programmes for clients including Tata Group, Mahindra Group, Aditya Birla Group and Godrej Group.

An industry luminary, she was chosen for the IMPACT Top 50 Women (2015, 2019, 2023), won Campaign India Mentor of the Year and Women Leading Change of the Year 2023 and was on the Cannes Lions Design Jury in 2018. Lulu champions women in leadership, mentors young women and teaches at top business schools. A polyglot and philanthropist, Lulu lives in Mumbai with her husband, Harsha, and two daughters, Ruhi and Riva.